Could You Be Startin' From Somewhere Else?

SKETCHES FROM BUFFALO AND BEYOND

*CARL,
TO ME WHO STILL
REMEMBERS BOW ANTHE
PLE!*

by Michael W. Shurgot

*SINCERELY,
[signature]
1/5/13*

ISBN: 1495248909
ISBN-13: 9781495248900
Library of Congress Control Number: 2014901222
CreateSpace Independent Publishing Platform
North Charleston, South Carolina

To:

The memory of my parents
William James Shurgot, 1910–1975
Mary Gertrude Spitzig Shurgot, 1914–2007

My sisters
Mary Lee Shurgot Brand
Anne Helen Shurgot Martin
and
their descendants

My wife
Gail Stumvoll Shurgot

Our children
Mara Catherine Shurgot Makel
Nicholas Michael Shurgot
and
their descendants

ACKNOWLEDGMENTS

This memoir began at midnight on December 27, 2007 after I finished reading Roger Angell's marvelous *Let Me Finish*. My wife, Gail, gave me Angell's memoir for Christmas, and once I began reading it I could not stop. Finishing Angell's book paradoxically made me ponder where I had begun: on the other side of New York State in a lower-middle-class neighborhood in a primarily industrial city where my childhood was vastly different from Mr. Angell's. My parents were not famous writers or editors, and their tastes were modest and pedestrian; they did not socialize with famous (or even infamous) intellectuals, and we did not have a second home in the Berkshires, the Hamptons, or anywhere else. Nonetheless, my childhood was emotionally rich and tremendously stimulating, and although I am not famous, do not have a public persona, and would be considered by "high society" to have come from "ordinary people," I believe that the stories of people from such ordinary backgrounds are worth telling. Think of this narrative as what my friend Joe Rautenstrauch called it, "a memoir of Everyman."

The other book that strongly influenced mine is Richard White's *Remembering Ahanagran: Storytelling in a Family's Past*. When I told my Irish friend Jim O'Donnell that I was taking a memoir-writing class at the University of Washington, he highly recommended White's book. White recounts his mother's life in Ireland and her subsequent settling in America, and he illuminates the ceaseless interplay between historical sources, such as family records and immigration data, and the remembered stories we tell about ourselves. I thank Jim for sending me to this terrific memoir.

My sister, Mary Lee, who lives in Williamsville, a suburb of Buffalo, was indispensable to this memoir. She has an astonishing memory, far better than mine, and I am profoundly in her debt for much of the history embedded in these sketches. Mary Lee created the maps of the neighborhood, and to my astonishment, she remembered most of the families on our block. She also has an extensive collection of family photographs and documents, including many photos of our parents that I had never seen, and I am immensely grateful to her for sharing this information. I thank her daughter, Jennifer, for her many hours spent rummaging around in Buffalo's libraries, researching vital pieces of the city's history. I also thank my sister, Anne, for her recollections of life with Mother and Father in Canton, Ohio, after they left Buffalo in the spring of 1966.

For suggestions about revisions of early drafts, I thank James Stark of Seattle and Martha and Richard Nochimson of New York. I am grateful to Lori Stephens of Verbatim Editorial for superb editorial assistance and to Gaines Hill and the design team at Create Space.

Kind permission to quote from *The Seafarer* by Conor McPherson was given by Nick Hern Books: www.nickhernbooks. co.uk.

Finally, I extend heartfelt gratitude to my forever Buffalo buddies: Paul Fiutak, Joe Rautenstrauch, Larry Riester, Kevin Reyner, Lenny Wiltburger, George Singleton (wherever he may be), Mike Kelly, Dick Olday, and (in memoriam) Dick Frucella. Together we forged deep and abiding friendships that animate many of the latter pages of this memoir.

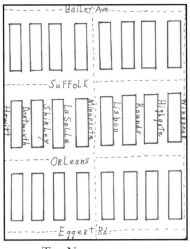

THE NEIGHBORHOOD

CONTENTS

Life is tough and brimming with loss, and the most we can do about it is to glimpse ourselves clear now and then, and find out what we feel about familiar scenes and recurring faces this time around.

Roger Angell, *Let Me Finish* (p. 2)

We all come from the past, and children ought to know what it was that went into their making, to know that life is a braided cord of humanity stretching up from time long gone, and that it cannot be defined by the span of a single journey from diaper to shroud.

Russell Baker, *Growing Up* (p. 8)

We turn our lives into stories, and, in doing so, we can stop them where we choose. Our stories do in a small way what memoirs and autobiographies do on a grander scale: they allow a self-fashioning that gives remembered lives a coherence that the day-to-day lives of actual experience lack.

Richard White, *Remembering Ahanagran* (p. 292)

In the early stages of creation of both art and science, everything in the mind is a story.

Edward O. Wilson, *The Social Conquest of Earth* (p. 275)

PROLOGUE:
A EULOGY FOR MOTHER

My mother died on January 5, 2007, three months after her ninety-second birthday. At her funeral at Infant of Prague Catholic Church in Buffalo, I gave the following eulogy.

The word *eulogy* in Greek means "good words." One reciting a eulogy is expected to speak words of praise about the deceased, but to speak as many words as would be necessary to summarize adequately my mother's life would be impossible, even impertinent. How ironic; Mother never stopped talking! That characteristic, however, propelled her energetic journey on this earth. My father was not given to many words, probably because Mother seldom gave him a chance to talk, but one statement he made about her was amazingly prescient. After they had been married for about fifteen years, Father said one day of Mother: "She detests peace and quiet!" How true.

MOTHER FEEDING SQUIRRELS; CHRISTMAS 2000, BUFFALO

The word that I would use to summarize my childhood home is *bedlam*. Life on Highgate Avenue was a constant jumble of disparate people: spirited Irish relatives, uncles arguing about baseball, aunts debating politics and fashion, Mr. and Mrs. Dressel from across the street looking for their three sons (who spent more time in our house than in theirs), a suddenly destitute friend crashing on the living room couch and staying for months, my friends Joe and Paul welcomed late on Sunday nights for tea, my sister Mary Lee's growing family, sharing and enlivening the rickety old house, and our younger sister Anne's friends from Holy Angels Academy. And pets: dogs, often two, cats, two or three, parakeets, fish, mice, rabbits, and ducks. Yes, ducks! I shall never forget the Saturday night that my father walked into the bathroom expecting a long, warm rest in the tub only to discover that his bath water, drawn slowly from the creaky plumbing, was inhabited by two ducks. Mother calmly explained that the ducks needed a swim and Father's bath could wait. I shall not repeat in this sanctuary the words that escaped my father's lips that night.

What seemed lunatic to everyone else seemed wonderful to Mother. She embraced what our neighbors—all fine, sane people—hated: Buffalo's fabled winter weather, which Mother cherished in direct proportion to its calamity. I remember old Mrs. Stegmans standing across the street, hip deep in snow during another blizzard, yelling at Mother, "This is your fault! You like this weather, don't you? You ordered this!" As if Mother could command the elements. She animated the world around her, and she taught all who accompanied her on her astonishing journey to appreciate every second, every minute, every hour, and every day of every year.

Mother was marvelously generous. A dinner party was successful in direct proportion to the number of people crammed into our house. If Mother suggested a picnic or a drive to the beach, we were encouraged to invite friends, so often half the neighborhood came along. Many a winter morning, when the postman arrived at our side door bearing his heavy sack and weary from trudging through deep snow, Mother invited him into the kitchen and served him a shot or two of Irish whiskey to warm his body and fortify him for the rest of his chilly journey. This was also Mother's way of gathering gossip from the postman about her Protestant neighbors, about whom she was always suspicious.

Mother lived as she did because she did not want to miss *anything* that life offered her. From the music of J. S. Bach to Saint Patrick's Day parades to ducks in the bathtub, all was part of the relentless circus that was the life of Mary Gertrude O'Hollaran Spitzig Shurgot. Often when I visited her in Buffalo during her final years, she was sitting in her room watching television while simultaneously listening to classical music on her favorite Canadian station. I thought her mad; how could one do both and comprehend either? Surely this was Mother's way, *in her nineties*, of embracing all that she could, whether it was a rerun of a 1950s comedy like *The Honeymooners* or *I Love Lucy,* classical music on the radio, or both simultaneously. Indeed, during her final hours, my daughter, Mara, my sisters, Anne and Mary Lee, and Mary Lee's daughters, Jennifer and Lisa, brought to the hospital a small radio with an earphone that they placed in Mother's ear so that as she lay dying she could hear one more concert.

My mother's spirit is now upstairs, and even as we gather here, I can imagine her raising, if you will pardon the expression, holy hell about something. The coffee isn't hot enough, the Guinness isn't cold enough, there aren't enough peanut-butter-and-jelly sandwiches or chocolate chip cookies, God hasn't scheduled enough storms for the coming winter (surely angels can be convinced to love snow!), or there isn't enough Irish music. Memo to Saint Peter: If you think you have your hands full now, just wait until Saint Patrick's Day. You had better have the pipes ready and the fiddles tuned, or believe me, you will hear from her.

I shall close with one short poem and a few lines from another. The first, "All Souls Night," is by the English poet Frances Cornford. Mother kept a copy of this poem taped to her refrigerator, and after Father died, she read it every evening as a reminder of the moment when, she believed, they would be reunited.

> My love came back to me
> Under the November tree
> Shelterless and dim.
> He put his hand upon my shoulder,
> He did not think me strange or older,
> Nor I, him.

The second is very different. Mother loved the poetry of Ireland and Wales, including Dylan Thomas, whose magical "A Child's Christmas in Wales" was always heard in our home during the holidays. Thomas wrote "Do Not Go Gentle into That Good Night" to his dying father, and by changing *father* to *mother* in the final stanza, I shall conclude this eulogy with four lines that capture my mother's fierce determination to live long and hard and to the max.

And you, my mother, there on that sad height,
Curse, bless me now with your fierce tears, I pray.
Do not go gentle into that good night.
Rage, rage, against the dying of the light. (lines 16–19)

That's a synopsis. The following pages fill out the story.

INTRODUCTION:
A PHOTO, A SETTING, AN ERA

I begin with an undated photograph taken at Alston Studios in Buffalo. Its date is less important than what it reveals about the short, bashful kid from Highgate I evoke in this memoir. I was born in 1943. From 1948 to 1957, I attended Saint Aloysius Gonzaga School in Cheektowaga, a suburb east of Buffalo, and this photo

THE AUTHOR, 1956 OR 1957

may have been taken for a seventh- or eighth-grade yearbook, alas now lost. In 1957, I entered Canisius High School, and I wore braces my first year there. This photo might have been taken during my freshman year.

Consider first the clothes. I seldom had my own. My father's older brother, Frank, had a son, Craig, who was two years older than I and also short. Throughout elementary school and Canisius, which had a strict jacket-shirt-tie dress code, I wore many of Craig's hand-me-downs. Note how mismatched this outfit is: the plaid jacket that is obviously too big in the shoulders with lapels far too wide, the shirt with the ridiculously long collars, and the bowtie with the Celtic knot design that clashes with the plaid of the jacket. This jacket was brown and green, the shirt light tan, and the bowtie pink and yellow. (Imagine this photo in color!) I attempt to appear content and self-possessed even as I am oblivious to the clashing, ill-fitting clothes. As a college literature professor, I always dressed stylishly, right down to the button-down Oxford shirts, paisley ties, and Harris

Tweed jackets. (Oh so British!) Perhaps my professional attire was a subconscious response to my memory of this photo.

The glasses indicate the poor eyesight that plagued my formative years, and the braces suggest how unattractive I thought myself when a young man is supposed to be developing "social graces." I was terribly shy around girls, partly because of the glasses, buck teeth, and oddly shaped jaw. All through elementary and high school, my mother told me that the glasses would make me look "very smart" (I withhold judgment on that proclamation) and that the braces would straighten my jaw and make me appear handsome. Well, maybe. Finally, note the comb in the breast pocket of the jacket. What was I thinking? Comb a crew cut?

The crew cut, the comb, and the tidy appearance reveal an early obsession for neatness and order. This obsession took many forms, and I recall one especially revealing example. By age four or five, I had accumulated a substantial collection of stuffed animals: a teddy bear, a giraffe, a cat, a dog, a squirrel, perhaps a tiger or a lion, and a few others. Every night when I got into bed, I arranged these companions in a neat row from my left shoulder to the edge of the bed, and in winter I ensured that the animals were under the covers so they would not get cold. Every night, I rotated the animals so that each one got its turn sleeping next to me. I insisted on this orderly rotation and thought it fair; each animal got the opportunity to be close to me, and if I rotated them, no animal was deprived of its share of my attention and would never feel slighted.

This sleeping rotation was important to me, and when my mother suggested that one of the animals was getting ragged, I protested that if one of my companions were discarded, the others would miss it, and the sleeping order that I had established would be disrupted. I have no idea how long I preserved this menagerie, but I know that I surgically repaired several crumbling members with tape, string, paper clips, staples, and safety pins. I couldn't part with any of these ragtag companions, just as, today, I keep for years a paint-splattered denim shirt hanging in the basement or lovingly tape the cover of a paperback book that I bought in 1967.

I also became obsessed with doodling the number eight. Still am. Composed of twin reversible, tangent circles enclosing finite spaces, this number has long symbolized a life of order and security that I deeply cherish.

I grew up in a conservative America that from the mid-1940s to the early 1960s was profoundly different from today's society. The roles of men and women were set; boys pursued professional careers, and girls became housewives and mothers. White people approved segregation, because it kept blacks and other minorities "in their place." Challenging American involvement in a war was unthinkable, and the enormous social upheavals of the civil rights era and the environmental movement were barely visible. Children did not have the Internet, cellphones, smartphones, iPods, and iPads to entertain them. They relied on their imaginations to create games in the streets and in their backyards that today seem silly. Boys raced from one end of the block to the other climbing neighbors' garages, and they fabricated baseball games, called "Strike Out," played by four kids on a vacant field. Boys got Lincoln Logs, Erector Sets, Tinker Toys, and Lionel Trains for Christmas, and girls got dollhouses. Boys traded Pops bubblegum baseball cards to collect their favorite team. (I had the entire 1957 World Series Champion Milwaukee Braves, with *two* Hank Aaron cards. Today that collection would be worth a fortune! Mother threw out my collection when I left Buffalo for graduate school in August, 1965). Boys used Butch Hair Wax and Brylcreem to plaster hair to their scalps, and the incessant whirling of Hula-Hoops ruined girls' hips and made fortunes for orthopedic surgeons. Timmy and Lassie, Sky King, and The Musketeers entertained millions of American children after school on black-and-white TVs. Gas was twenty-five cents a gallon; Studebakers, as ugly as the Ford Edsel, roamed America's streets like alien spaceships; and Burma Shave signs lined American highways. We lived with terrible fears during the Cold War and practiced ducking under our desks at school, pretending that we would be protected from nuclear annihilation.

Technical innovation and social change were evident. The Bendix G-15, one of the earliest mass-produced computers, was introduced in 1956 and weighed 950 pounds. Drive-in restaurants featured carhops in sexy, two-piece outfits, riding around parking lots on roller skates. Drive-in movies, where couples could make out as they pleased in privacy, hastened the sexual revolution of the 1960s. The first McDonald's opened in 1955 and sold hamburgers for fifteen cents. Recording artists Fats Domino, Little Richard, Bo Diddley, Bill Haley & His Comets, Chuck Berry, Della Reese, Sam Cooke, Chubby Checker, The Temptations, The Everly Brothers, Buddy Holly and the Crickets, The Four Seasons, and Elvis Presley transformed American popular music, and many black musicians burst into musical prominence. In 1957, Dick Clark began hosting *American Bandstand* from Los Angeles on ABC, propelling rock and roll and rhythm and blues into every American home. In 1959, Miles Davis recorded *Kind of Blue*, the best-selling album in jazz history. In 1955, the Brooklyn Dodgers, led by the brilliant Jackie Robinson, who smashed baseball's insidious color barrier in 1947, miraculously beat the New York Yankees in the World Series and proved that underdogs could finally be victorious in America.

Buffalo has historically been home to large numbers of European immigrants, and during my childhood, the city's neighborhoods, which Mark Goldman remarks resembled "medieval villages each with their own churches, markets, and water supply," were dominated by residents who cherished their ethnic identities. The Bailey-Kensington neighborhood in northeastern Buffalo included primarily German and Polish families, most of the West Side from Main Street to the Niagara River was Italian, south Buffalo and the First Ward were fiercely Irish, and Poles and Germans dominated the East Side from Main Street across the Lovejoy and Broadway-Fillmore neighborhoods. Other European immigrants, including Slovaks, Romanians, Hungarians, Serbians, Brits, Scotts, Dutch, and Swedes, established neighborhoods in North Buffalo and the suburbs of Williamsville, Amherst, and Kenmore.

These immigrants were drawn to Buffalo because of its rapid industrial development, beginning in the late nineteenth century. In 1905, an article in *Buffalo Times* stated that since 1890, 412 new factories had been built within the city, and $137 million had been invested in industrial production. Burgeoning factories included Buffalo and Susquehanna Iron Company, Urban Flour Mill, Snow Steam Pump Works, Buffalo Foundry Company, Buffalo Structural Steel Company, and Lackawanna Iron and Steel Company, which in 1904 opened a gigantic, sprawling factory that still rusts along Lake Erie. Encouraged by extensive shipping facilities and railroad links across the nation, milling, grain elevators, and later automobile and chemical companies flocked to Buffalo and Western New York. By 1910, more than ten thousand men worked in 150 iron and steel factories in Buffalo, 3,600 people worked in the automobile industry, 3,400 in the manufacture and repair of railroad equipment, and 1,800 in copper manufacturing.

This industrial growth continued into World War II. In 1943, 104 war-related industries operated in Buffalo, including Frederick Flater, General Electric, Sylvania Electric, and Sterling Engine Company, all industries in which my father worked. Foundries and steel plants employed tens of thousands of workers, including many African Americans, whose population in Buffalo reached 24,000 by 1945. Most residents assumed that the city's prosperity and its tradition of tightly knit, homogeneous neighborhoods would continue, but within a few years after World War II, Buffalo was changing. The nearly exclusive ethnic populations of many neighborhoods, coupled with the growing black population that was drawn to the city by high employment in the war years, generated discriminatory policies in city government, public education, major industries, and real estate markets. These policies limited black employment and incursions into ethnic enclaves and the integration of public schools. Several disastrous attempts at urban renewal (including the infamous Ellicott Urban Renewal Project, which demolished an entire neighborhood on the east side in the early 1950s, and the annihilation of Humboldt Parkway and its majestic trees in 1958 to build the Kensington Expressway) exacerbated the city's social fragmentation.

The opening of the Saint Lawrence Seaway in 1959 crippled Buffalo's heretofore central position as a shipping hub and devastated many waterfront industries. Between 1954 and 1967, manufacturing employment in Buffalo and Western New York declined from 180,000 to 154,000, and "white flight" to the suburbs hastened the rapid decline in the city's population. In 1950, it was 532,000, but on January 2, 2010, it was 268,900. Suburban shopping malls catered to predominantly white customers, while many small businesses with ethnic identities—family-run Polish markets, Italian restaurants, German pastry shops, and Irish pubs—closed, along with neighborhood schools and churches. Decreasing population, shrinking economic activity, high unemployment, and segregated housing hastened the city's decline.

During his tenure at the University of Buffalo, English Professor Leslie Fiedler famously asserted that Buffalo exhibited "the phosphorescence of decay." Ironically enough, during Fiedler's tenure, the Buffalo Bills, led by their ferocious fullback, Cookie Gilchrist, won the 1964 and 1965 championship games in the upstart American Football League. The 1964 championship game was played at Buffalo's decrepit War Memorial Stadium, aka The Rock Pile, and attracted 40,713 fans. Today, the Bills play in the American Conference of the National Football League, but their home field, Ralph Wilson Stadium, is in Orchard Park, west of Buffalo. Even the city's best known professional franchise moved to the suburbs.

This was the era and the setting of my photo. Despite its often bleak history, Buffalo was, and is, home, and thence I return. The subtitle of this book is "Sketches from Buffalo and Beyond" because rather than narrating cohesive, carefully sequenced events, the following chapters evoke a home, a neighborhood, an extended family, vivid memories, and enduring friendships in a somewhat jumbled fashion. We hope that from within our stories coherence emerges, yet our lives are a kaleidoscope where memory and history tumble together and yield constantly different visions. What follows are the visions that have emerged, in Roger Angell's phrase, this time around.

Chapter 1:
A House on Highgate

Mother's favorite Irish joke, which she told every Saint Patrick's Day, goes something like this.

Late on an autumn afternoon, Paddy and Mike are sitting together at Mann's 300 Club on Bailey Avenue, each sipping his second Guinness. After a moment, Mike says to Paddy, "Paddy, I'm needin' to get to Smitty's. It's up on Kensington, I think, near Eggert Road. I'm supposed to meet Tim there for dinner at six. What's the best way?"

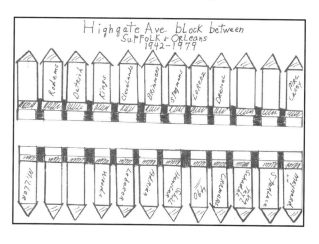

"Well," says Paddy, staring into his glass. "Give me a moment on that one." After a few more sips, he says, "Well, Mike, you go out here and turn left onto Bailey Avenue. You go two blocks, and I think you'll come to Lisbon Avenue. Turn left, go one block, then right again onto probably Suffolk Avenue, then two more blocks, or is it three? Well anyway, you keep going until you hit a stoplight, which I think is at Dartmouth Avenue, and then turn, wait, or go straight? Which is it now? Let me think about this some more."

Paddy takes a draught of his Guinness and then gently lays his pint on the bar. A moment later, he says smartly to Mike, "I got it! Ignore that last set of directions. Here's what you do. You go out o' the bar, and instead of turning left, you go right. Go one block, turn right again. That'll put you on Winspear Avenue.

You go two blocks, turn right, and then you're on Orleans Avenue. Forget about Suffolk. You go down Orleans for about five blocks, turn left, I think, onto LaSalle Avenue. Well, then you turn left again, and this takes you to Eggert Road, but as to which way you turn there I am, bless me mother, not quite sure."

"Well," says Mike, somewhat exasperated, "Could you be giving me directions you might be sure about?"

Paddy tips his glass and takes a long draught. Finally, he says, "Well now, here's a third try. Go out the bar, and get onto Highgate. It's just right around the corner here. Go down Highgate to Suffolk, where them kids are always playin' football when you're tryin' to park your car, and where I was meaning to send you all along, and go right, but don't go as far as Dartmouth. There's no damn light there. The light is at Shirley Avenue. Turn left. I'm sure it is Shirley where the light is. Go to Orleans, and turn right. You go all the way to Kensington Avenue, and then you turn, oh damn, is it left or right? Now give me a minute on that part."

Paddy drains his pint. Stroking his chin, he looks calmly at Mike and asks, "Could you be startin' from somewhere else?"

—⁂—

Well, no. No one starts from somewhere else. A few years ago, at a social gathering in Seattle, a new acquaintance, obviously "well heeled" as my mother used to say, asked me where I was from.

"Buffalo," I said enthusiastically.

"Oh," he said. "I'm *so* sorry."

"I'm not," I said and stomped away. I have never been sorry that I started in Buffalo.

My story starts in June 1943 in a small clapboard house at 490 Highgate Avenue, between Suffolk and Orleans, a mostly middle-class neighborhood of two-lane streets in the Bailey-Kensington neighborhood, part of the University District in the extreme northeast corner of the city. The main drag, Bailey Avenue, ran north-south and was bound at one end by Kensington Avenue and at the other by Main Street. To the east was Eggert Road, which paralleled Bailey and marked the city's eastern boundary. Beyond Eggert Road were the suburbs of Cheektowaga, Amherst, and Williamsville, where people drove Buicks and Cadillacs and lived in brick houses, which to me symbolized wealth. At the corner of Eggert Road and Kensington Avenue, the southeast corner of the neighborhood, was a small shopping plaza where boys ventured on bikes to "look at girls" who frequented there. One block east of our house was Public School 80, and on long summer nights, I gathered there with other kids to play softball. On both sides of Bailey Avenue, going north to Main Street, were vast green fields that in my imagination beckoned heroic deeds. On one side was the Grover Cleveland Golf Course, where in summer we waded into ponds to collect golf balls that we resold at the first tee, and where in winter we played hockey on the frozen ponds. Across from the golf course, on the University of Buffalo campus at the intersection of Bailey Avenue and Main Street, was a large open field to which we rode our bikes and transformed into Ebbets Field or Yankee Stadium for endless baseball games.

The neighborhood was mostly residential but included numerous small businesses on both sides of Bailey Avenue. Unlike the chain stores and franchises that dominate shopping plazas in most American cities today, the shops on Bailey were mostly independent, and the owners knew their customers well. Although Mother shopped weekly at the large Nu-Way Grocery Store near Saint Aloysius Church in Cheektowaga, she also patronized several specialty stores on Bailey. She purchased Friday night's fish at Schneider's Oyster Company, near the corner of Bailey and LaSalle; fresh bread and baked goods at Breimer's Bake Shop at Bailey and Lisbon; and fancy meats and cheeses at Mueller's Delicatessen, also near Lisbon. Taylor's Shoe Repair near Stockbridge surgically prolonged the life of shoes and winter boots, and at the Deco Restaurant at the corner of Bailey and East Amherst, Mother stopped for coffee and treated us to hot chocolate on wintry days. Near Hewitt Avenue and Bailey was a Goodyear Service Station, where Father bought tires for his cars. Every December I paid a dollar there for an album of Christmas music that featured holiday tunes like "Sleigh Ride" and "Walking in a Winter Wonderland" performed by the Andre Kostelanetz Orchestra, the Ray Conniff Singers, the Nelson Riddle Orchestra, and Arthur Fiedler and the Boston Pops, and carols by the Mormon Tabernacle Choir, Fred Warring and the Pennsylvanians, and the Robert Shaw Choral.

Mother sent Mary Lee to Lisbon-Bailey Drugs for cold medicines and toiletries and the clerks, who knew Mother well and trusted her, added the cost to Mother's bill and sent Mary Lee home with a receipt. Mother shopped for kids' clothes at the Wee-Tog Infants Shop and for herself and Father at F. W. Woolworth department store. (At the five-and-dime store next to F. W. Woolworth, there was a cashier with half of a right arm, probably a victim of the polio virus that every parent dreaded. We marveled while watching her remove dollar bills from the cash machine with her left hand; she then pinned the bills under her right elbow as she removed coins and gave us the proper change with her left hand.) We had our sweaters and winter coats cleaned at Buffalo Dry Cleaners, bought small appliances and had them repaired at Hack's Electrical Appliances, and at Frontier Hobbies near Berkshire Avenue I spent endless hours deciding which freight cars to buy for my Lionel model train. At the corner of Bailey and Rounds was a small grocery store, owned by Italian immigrants, where we returned pop bottles for the five-cent deposit, and my friends and I bought packages of Topps bubblegum that included treasured baseball cards.

Bailey boasted several bars (my father and Uncle Frank called them "grog shops") such as Metzger's Lounge, Keller's Tavern near LaSalle, and Mann's Three Hundred Club at Bailey and Highgate where Paddy and Mike were known to spend a wee bit of time. A few doors down from Frontier Hobbies was the Kensington Liquor Store where Father bought Ballantine's Scotch and Four Roses, and Mother bought Jameson Irish Whiskey for Saint Patrick's Day and rum for eggnog at Christmas.

Liberty Savings and Loan, on Bailey near Kensington, was the site for one of Mother's endearing rituals. Every Friday, she put on a fancy dress and white gloves and drove to Father's work place, picked up his check, and drove to Liberty Savings to deposit it. Mother apparently felt that Father's earning a decent income warranted an appropriately formal response. The thought of Mother, the elegantly attired guardian of her husband's earnings, delicately handing Father's check to a bank clerk suggested how much she valued her family's well-being. Automatic electronic deposits, while convenient and safer than transporting a personal check across town, have erased such memorable rituals and their symbolic connection to family life.

At 3165 Bailey, near Berkshire, was the neighborhood kids' favorite hangout, the Basil Brothers Varsity Theater. On Saturday afternoons, we paid a quarter and saw two full-length movies, usually a Western and a horror film or space thriller, and two Looney Tunes cartoons. We saw Westerns like *Rio Grande*, *Rawhide*, Gary Cooper's classic *High Noon*, the original *Lone Ranger*, *Gunfight at the O.K. Corral*, and "Indian movies" like *Last of the Comanches* where the Native Americans, always the bad guys, were slaughtered by the US Cavalry. We saw many "shoot-em-ups" with John Wayne as the archetypal Western hero and "singing Westerns" with Roy Rogers and Gene Autry. The horror films included numerous B-movie thrillers like *The Thing from Another World*, *The Beast from 20,000 Fathoms*, *Invasion of the Body Snatchers*, and classics like *Godzilla, King of the Monsters, Frankenstein,* and *The Mummy*. The cartoons often featured the cat-and-mouse games of "Tom & Jerry" or the Roadrunner's narrow escapes from Wily Coyote (who spent most of his life blowing himself up or slamming into rock walls). I gleaned from watching Wily that life could be hard. Walking home past the Carlton A. Ullrich Funeral Parlor on bleak, wintry Saturdays confirmed my suspicion of mortality.

On our block, most of the families were Polish or German, along with some Irish and Italian families, with names like Stegmans, Miller, Dressel, Dietrich, Brimmer, Hennsler, Casey, and Lorenz. Many of these families, like mine, included recent immigrants. For its day, I suppose that the neighborhood might have qualified as "multicultural," but in fact, like most of Buffalo during my childhood, it was rigidly segregated. There were few Jewish and no African American families in the Bailey-Kensington neighborhood until the late 1960s, and I never heard "Latino" used to describe Latin American immigrants, who lived in small, isolated clusters in the Lovejoy neighborhood well south of the University District. Like most white kids in Buffalo of the 1950s, regardless of their ethnicity, I had little contact with African Americans or Hispanics and less knowledge of the social consequences of prejudice in the larger city. For many years, I saw black people only when my father took me to see the AAA Buffalo Bisons of the International League play in Offerman Stadium, at the corner of Michigan Avenue and East Ferry Street. The stadium's seating patterns further isolated me from black people who seemed to live in an entirely different world, even though we lived in the same city.

Our house stood in the middle of the block, separated from adjacent houses by a narrow driveway through which one could barely, and carefully, drive a small sedan at five miles per hour; any faster was risky. A few larger houses up the street, like my friend Danny Miller's house, boasted wider driveways, an amenity that signaled bigger cars and upward social mobility. Most of the dwellings were two stories, often including multiple generations. In the Dressel house across the street, for example, my early companions, the brothers George, Paul, and Danny lived with their parents in the cramped upstairs flat while Mr. Dressel's churlish parents occupied the much-roomier downstairs. The neighborhood was densely populated, and on summer evenings, people sat outside on porches, listening to broadcasts of the Bisons and relishing the breezes wafting off Lake Erie that brought some relief from the oppressive heat and humidity. Greetings, sometimes in German or Polish, tumbled from porches to older residents or young parents walking by pushing baby carriages. When we denizens of the street insisted on prolonging our noisy games of stickball or touch football well past sundown, the greetings morphed into cries, usually in English, to "Knock it off!" When a really annoyed neighbor descended from his porch, we scattered.

Like many of the houses on our block, ours was crowded. My mother's sister, Katherine, bought the property in 1939, and my parents didn't buy it from her until 1951. For several years of our family's life on Highgate, my parents were renters, a fact that, as his young family grew, complicated Father's efforts to maintain property that he did not own. Katherine (Aunt Kay to me and my sisters) lived with us until she entered the Sisters of Saint Joseph convent in 1956. My mother's aunt, Nana Brown Flanigan, whose husband had served in World War I, also lived with us until she died in the small back bedroom in 1959. The flag we flew at the house on the Fourth of July, Veterans Day, and other civic occasions belonged to Nana's husband and symbolized the fierce patriotism of European immigrants in the early twentieth century. I never understood how Nana, as we called her, was related to our family, except that she was Irish. For much of my childhood I assumed that all Irish people were related and therefore obligated by this vast, complex web of blood ties to take in relatives once, twice, or thrice removed; the degree of separation was immaterial.

Being Irish, Mother loved to tell stories, and I am sure that many of the stories that she claimed were true were actually fanciful, but 'tis no matter. She constantly told us stories about her Irish relatives in Boston and the tales her grandmother told her about Ireland, including accounts of the "little people" that she heard as a child. The image of Ireland and the Irish people who captured my imagination as a small child was of this strange, misty land inhabited by people whose kin were everywhere and by fairies and leprechauns who might appear in our house and might even be related to us. I was convinced that these little people lived in the deep recesses of the attic or in the damp little rooms that Father built in the basement where every winter Mother stored dozens of Mason jars and bags of vegetables in wooden crates. Years later, in a class on modern poetry at Canisius College, I read Theodore Roethke's poem, "Root Cellar," and knew what the little people, surely vegetarians, must have been living on during those interminable Buffalo winters.

> Bulbs broke out of boxes hunting for chinks in the dark,
> Shoots dangled and drooped,
> Lolling obscenely from mildewed crates,
> Hung down long yellow evil necks, like tropical snakes. (lines 2–5)

'Twas a dangerous place, that cellar. I never entered without fear and a flashlight, though I was almost too frightened to turn it on. No space in our old house was unoccupied, by big or little people. As the family grew, its members shifted bedrooms and my parents bought bunk beds.

My sister, Mary Lee, or Mandy as Father called her, was born in 1945, and she and I shared a bedroom downstairs until our sister, Anne Helen, was born in 1950. My parents decided that the house needed an extra bedroom, so a year later Father began building what became my abode in the back of the attic. He built the entire room himself: erected the pine two-by-four framing, installed double-pane windows that looked out on the backyard and the neighborhoods beyond, wired the electrical work, installed heating ducts through the attic floor to the furnace, hung doors, carefully cut and laid the tile floor, installed corkboard and grooved panels floor to ceiling, and perfectly aligned the beveled woodwork that he painted fire-engine red.

To this day I, all thumbs, have no idea how my father created this room from the barren floor of the attic. Night after night and all day Saturdays I stood at the edge of his workbench in the basement, watching him measure and mark the wood. He mastered the screeching table saw that always cut exactly, because as he guided the wood he fed it with his fingers. I was sure that someday parts of several fingers would end up on the floor in a mess of bloody sawdust. He was a gifted craftsman and never lost as much as a fingernail to that whirling blade. I forever asked if I could help, and he always said, "This is a one-man job," a phrase that hinted at the distance that he maintained between himself and his children. When I became a father in my late twenties, I vowed that I would never utter that phrase to my children.

The room itself was about ten by ten. The door, set neatly in its red trim, opened into a modern version of a monk's medieval study. Everything I needed was here: a cozy bed, a closet overflowing with coats and sweaters mandated by Buffalo's fierce winters, a desk, and a bookcase crammed with my growing library. I moved into this room in the mid-1950s, before graduating from Saint Aloysius Gonzaga School in 1957, and it was my haunt throughout high school and college. Because my sisters shared a bedroom downstairs, I was the only member of the family with a room of my own, secluded in a space that my father magically created out of wood, tiles, glass, wires, metal, and love. The longer I lived in the room, the more it became a sanctuary, a necessary retreat from the noise and confusion of relatives, cats, dogs, ducks, and often incorrigible family feuds downstairs. I listened to Miles Davis and John Coltrane and read until the early morning hours, filling my imagination with a wealth of stories that rivaled Mother's Irish tales and eventually became my life's work.

For most of my childhood, I shared my bedroom with a forty pound black Labrador Retriever named Brandy. Mother named him that because of his deep-brown eyes and a streak of hair the color of brandy liqueur down his chest. On winter nights when the temperature hovered near zero, Brandy curled up at the foot of my bed, and because he always fell asleep before I got into bed and I could not budge him, I often slept in a fetal position, cocooned against the cold. During those long winter nights when my father turned down the furnace and the entire family slept under layers of Hudson Bay blankets, I had the additional comfort of a large, wooly dog who knew where to find a warm spot.

Although memory is a trickster that can both clarify and cloud one's reminiscence, I cling tenaciously to a vision that became central to my developing consciousness as a child. Of all the stories Mother read to us, Thomas's "A Child's Christmas in Wales" was the most captivating, and no holiday celebration was complete without it. In my early years, each time I heard or read Thomas's sensuous evocation of the white wonderland of a Welsh Christmas, I was convinced that he had once lived in Buffalo or that Buffalo had once been part of Wales—or both. Like Thomas in Wales, every winter in Buffalo I lived with the "muffling silence of the eternal snows." Eternal indeed; many an Easter my mother complained loudly to God for sending another snow storm that meant her children had to wear coats over their new clothes and ugly galoshes over their new shoes. In the final paragraph, Thomas describes Auntie Hannah's last songs on Christmas night, how everybody laughed, finally going to bed, and then this:

> Looking through my bedroom window, out into the moonlight and the unending smoke-colored snow, I could see the lights of all the other houses on our hill and hear the music rising from them up the long, steadily falling night. I turned the gas down, I got into bed, I said some prayers to the close and holy darkness, and then I slept. (p. 21)

During the long, cold winter nights of my childhood, often well past midnight, alone in the attic room with only a large, sleeping dog for company. I stood at my bedroom windows and gazed into the night that seemed eternally beautiful. Through the windows, I saw the houses of our neighborhood, row upon endless row, stretching into the darkness, each covered with fresh, deep snow that sparkled in the moonlight. I believed that the colder the air, the brighter the moonlight, and so the longer I gazed into the wintry night, the more I was enthralled by the brilliant light of the moon that pirouetted over the snowy rooftops. During such moments I felt wondrously alive, as if I were witnessing a shimmering miracle of snow and light that christened and cleansed the whole world, or at least my neighborhood. The words that Thomas would have said to the "close and holy darkness"—in the imaginations of children who live with winter, all nights are holy—were surely prayers of gratitude. He too, I believed, felt blessed to look out upon a dazzling winter's night that paradoxically felt more inviting than any summer scene could. I slept, with Brandy warming my feet, buried under many covers

MICHAEL AND MARY LEE; BACKYARD, DECEMBER, 1948

and enveloped by the beauty and solace of winter.

Such comforting, cozy nights convinced me when I was four or five that only the "real places" in the world experienced winter. Wales and Buffalo were real. Maybe Rochester, which wasn't far away, and parts of Pennsylvania, which was south of Buffalo and was regularly plastered by the "lake effect" that dumped huge amounts of snow on Western New York and northern Pennsylvania. Florida, which I often heard my parents and relatives mention, was not real. It could not possibly exist, and nobody could possibly live there because Florida never experienced winter. I would write a letter to Dylan Thomas and invite him to spend a winter with me in Buffalo so he could look out my windows on winter nights and see the snow glistening in the holy darkness. I was sure that Brandy would enjoy the company.

Given my parents' modest income during my early childhood, I learned to accept as normal what now seem like impossible inconveniences. Until at least 1949 we had no refrigerator; we had an icebox, an ancient contraption memorialized by the American poet William Carlos Williams in "This Is Just to Say" ("I have eaten / the plums / that were in / the icebox"). It was a squat, white rectangle with two steel drawers at the base for the ice. It stood in the northeast corner of the kitchen, near the windows that opened into the narrow driveway. I assumed that the icebox was part of the house when my parents moved in, because I have no memory of its being carried into the house.

Michael and Mary Lee; snowball warriors, December, 1948

But I do remember the ice man. Two to three times a week, depending on the season, he arrived in front of our house driving a small truck with ICE scrawled in huge letters across the side. He was an urban giant with immensely strong hands and bulging arms, and his predictable return became one of the rituals by which I measured the passage of time. He was always in a hurry, especially in summer, and announced his arrival half way up our driveway, yelling "Ice man! Ice man!" Without waiting to be invited inside, he opened the side door and barreled up the back stairs and into the kitchen, terrifying the sleeping cats in the living room and sending Brandy into a fit of barking until he left, despite Mother yelling, "Brandy, shut up! It's only the ice man! He was just here Tuesday!" In each hand, he carried steel tongs with which he squeezed huge chunks of ice that he carefully lowered into the cavernous drawers at the bottom of the box. He left as quickly as he entered, moving to his next customer, bearing his precious cargo.

The box was well insulated and designed to keep the ice frozen as long as possible. I can still hear my father intoning, "Close the icebox!" every time some-one reached into it to get food. This exhortation was his way of saving ice and hence money. As the ice melted, the drawers at the bottom filled with water, and when all the ice had melted my parents strenuously lifted them, cursing all the while how "goddamn heavy" they were, dragged them across the linoleum floor, and lifted and dumped them into the sink, thus preparing them for the ice man's return. The ice man arrived; the ice melted; the ice man returned. I developed a sense that living in this old house meant participating in larger natural processes of which we were a small but necessary part. My father told me that during the winters, when Lake Erie froze miles from shore, brave men with sharp saws ventured onto the ice, cut large chunks, and loaded them onto their trucks to deliver to iceboxes all over Buffalo. In the summer there was, somewhere in Buffalo, a gigantic factory that made ice and kept it frozen.

Because the icebox was next to the large kitchen windows and its capacity was limited, during the winter my mother stored food on the windowsill with the storm windows wide open. Mother loved winter and welcomed it into her house at every opportunity, and with what she considered judicious practicality she turned the kitchen window into a handy extension of the icebox. Given that contraption's severe space limitations, why not use the ten-degree nights to keep the milk and orange marmalade cold? Father, who every fall risked his life climb-ing a shaky wooden ladder to hang the storm windows, downstairs *and* upstairs, saw this situation differently. Leaving food on a windowsill with the storm window wide open was lunacy.

"Mary, for Christ's sake, close the pneumonia hole!"

"Oh, but Bill, the cold air feels good in here."

"It's ten degrees out there! You're making the whole house cold!"

"Well, the icebox is full, and this way the milk and juice and jam and butter will stay cold."

"All that can stay on the kitchen table. None of it has to be kept cold. Close the damn window! Why the hell do you think I install storm windows every fall?"

"Well, I'll leave it open just a little then."

And so on. Father wandered around the house all winter, muttering about heavy wooden ladders and open storm windows and heating bills, while on most winter days my sisters and I returned from school to a chilly kitchen and jars of jam and jelly and bottles of milk and orange juice sitting on the window sill. Every Thanksgiving Mother cooked a feast and after dinner stored the remaining turkey and apple and pumpkin pies on the open sill, explaining to Father that the cool autumn air refreshed the kitchen and initiating their four-month battle about open storm windows and heating bills. I will never know why the turkey and pies stored on the windowsill were never eaten by squirrels or birds. Luck of the Irish, maybe. Acquiring a refrigerator upgraded our living standards, but that icebox remains a fixture in my memory of home the way an electric refrigerator never could. When the ice man stopped coming, an important ritual of my early childhood disappeared.

The original furnace was a coal burner, a truly monstrous machine that in its size, noise, and burning interior was as fascinating as it was frightening. When roaring, it seemed on the verge of exploding, yet without it I knew we could never survive a Buffalo winter, especially the ones that lasted from early November to mid-April. Whereas the ice man charged into our kitchen two to three times a week, the coal man's singular arrival was *the* harbinger of winter. As burly as the ice man and smeared from head to toe with soot, the coal man backed his truck into the narrow driveway, pulled a curved metal chute from beneath the load of coal, and poked it through the hinged casement below the kitchen windows. He opened a door in the back of the truck, and coal cascaded into a holding bin in the cellar, sending up swirling dust clouds that inundated much of the basement and imperiled breathing. If Brandy or the cats were sleeping in the basement when the coal crashed through the casement, they yelped and screeched and scattered up the stairs into the kitchen, startled by the noise and dust that enveloped them.

Because we did not have a clothes dryer for many years, and on rainy days Mother had to hang clothes in the basement, if the coal man arrived while linens and sheets were drying calamity ensued. The clotheslines were strung behind the furnace to take advantage of its heat but precariously close to the coal bin. Although the coal man usually made his first delivery during the last two weeks of October, Mother frequently failed to anticipate his arrival. If on a washing day she heard the coal truck's grinding gears rattling windows as it backed into the narrow driveway, she raced downstairs, hurling venomous curses at the poor man who was only trying to do his job.

"Michael, Mandy, Anne, the coal man is here! Grab the baskets and help me get the wash down! I just washed the sheets and hung them! They'll get filthy! Why the hell does he have to come on a wash day? Damn it!"

Careening down the stairs, we collided with the menagerie charging up the stairs, eliciting Mother's rage —"You lousy cats, move!"—as she dashed toward the back of the basement where her clean white wash disappeared in clouds of coal dust.

This huge pile of coal was vaguely terrifying: it arrived with hideous noise; it came, like the ice in summer, from places I could not fathom; and it defiantly occupied its own forbidding corner of the cellar. After the coal arrived, my father opened a door at the corner of the bin closest to the furnace and used a shovel to distribute the pile evenly. When he handed me a shovel and invited me inside the bin to help him, I felt that I had been invited to participate in an essential task that only men could perform. It was, I suppose, a rite of passage, although I doubt my father thought about the health risks of asking a boy to climb around a mound of coal. I neither thought nor cared about the coal dust; this was not a one-man job but one that a son could do with his father. That was enough; the black dust on my face and clothes when I walked upstairs was a sign of manhood. Let it snow! Let it freeze! The coal was securely embedded in the basement, and I had helped prepare our house for another long winter.

Like the ice man, the coal man eventually disappeared from Highgate. Neither the plug-in refrigerator nor the oil tank, both of which arrived in the early 1950s, involved memorable rituals. The glitzy refrigerator hummed along all by itself. It didn't require thrice-weekly visits by a burly man bearing iron claws, it obviated the need to store turkeys and pies and jam on the windowsill, and it silenced one of the more memorable disputes between my parents about the usefulness of storm windows. The oil man arrived periodically in a shiny truck during winter to pump oil into the newly installed tank where the ghastly coal bin had stood. He parked his truck at the curb, stuck his hose through the open casement, and quietly filled the tank. One of the more bizarre recurrences of my childhood was thus lost: yelping dogs, screeching cats, and a load of coal thundering into the basement, all to the tune of curses hurled from above as Mother frantically tried to rescue a week's wash.

The obvious alternative to drying clothes in the cellar was drying them in the backyard where Father had also strung several clotheslines. Most Mondays, Mother, Mandy, and I lugged into the backyard baskets of wet clothes that Mother had put through the washing machine's manual ringer. Only rain, not cold, prevented Mother from drying clothes outside; as long as the sun was shining, even in winter, we trudged outside with our heavy baskets to hang the wash. In typical winter temperatures, the damp clothes froze. Helping Mother fold frozen sheets while standing in several inches of snow seemed nutty, especially as I usually had to shovel a path to the backyard before we could even get there. This exercise got us outside, weather be damned, and Mother remarked on how "fresh" our clothes, though frozen solid, smelled after being hung outside. Considering this weekly ritual, and the health benefits that Mother insisted came with having clothes and sheets hung in the crisp winter air, one can imagine how furious she was if she had a week's washing drying or thawing in the basement when the unholy coal man arrived and filled the cellar with soot.

During the summer months, another intrepid entrepreneur regularly visited the neighborhood: the "rag man." Sitting proudly on a narrow, worn plank on top of his horse-drawn wagon, the heavy-set man, wearing shabby clothes and sporting a greasy top hat, crowed, "Rags today! Rags today! Give us your rags! Rags today!" as his horse hobbled down Highgate. Rag men collected virtually any household paraphernalia—used clothes, old pots and pans, shoes, even small appliances—that they could sell elsewhere in the city, probably to charities. Mother kept in the basement a pile of what she called rags—old clothes, frayed rugs, thread-bare sheets, and towels or old cotton shirts—and when she heard the rag man hollering she ran to the basement, gathered and bundled her collection, and told us to carry it all to the curb where we hurled the bundle onto the man's cart. We thought him immensely peculiar; why would anyone ride around on a rickety cart drawn by a decrepit horse and actually collect other people's junk, things even he called "rags"?

The Dressel boys and I teased him unmercifully. When we saw him coming, we ran up the street to him and walked next to his cart yelling, "Rags-rags your own self!" at the poor old man. One day, exasperated by our teasing, he jumped off his wagon and chased us halfway down the block. "You lousy little brats! I'll show you! Think you're so smart, do ya? Come here! Pick on an old man, will ya?"

Terrified, we ran to my house and hid in the basement behind the coal bin. God only knows what he would have done had he caught us. Maybe he would have tied us in a sack and hurled us onto his wagon to become another bundle of rags that he hauled around town. We stayed in our basement for several hours, afraid that he was waiting for us in the backyard or hiding behind his horse. We never teased him again.

I have no idea what happened to the rag man or who, or what, replaced him. Pickup trucks from Goodwill? When a rag man died, did he have a son who took his route? A brother? Like the ice man and the coal man, one day the rag man disappeared from Highgate and from my childhood. Was I conscious of the last visit of any of these itinerant workmen? I think not, though I wish now that I had been, because in my memory their ritual appearances remain amazingly vivid. The ice man and the coal man were huge, hulking figures who dressed in what Father called "work clothes": heavy, steel-toed Red Wing boots, grubby flannel or denim shirts, dungarees so soiled with grime and caked with dirt that Mother said when removed they would stand up by themselves, and thick leather gloves. I especially remember the ice man's gloves. Creases were worn into the leather from carrying tongs day after day, and they fit so tightly that I imagined the creases were worn into his hands. I wondered if he could even remove the gloves and had to wear them while he slept. Such were the uniforms that these men wore, proudly identifying themselves, their trade, and their importance to the neighborhood.

Where did such men go when refrigerators, oil-burning furnaces, and Goodwill trucks obliterated their livelihoods? I realize now that their demise was but one small part of inevitable economic and social changes happening all around me about which, as a child, I was oblivious. I knew only that I cherished Mother's cursing, the yelping menagerie, and the clamor and confusion that the ice man and especially the coal man created. The house itself seemed to treasure the bedlam. Conversely, the refrigerator hummed quietly, the oil truck driver parked at the curb and calmly filled the tank, and every few months a man from Goodwill called ahead to ask for donations that we left on the curb the night before. Technology brought us a quieter but less vital existence.

Before Father bought a television in 1953, the principal entertainment in our house was the tall Philco radio console in the dining room. From a young age, I was fascinated by the voices that regularly entered our house. Throughout the baseball season, announcers' monologues echoed from room to room: Mel Allen, the voice of the New York Yankees from Yankee Stadium; Red Barber, who called the Yankees and later the Brooklyn Dodgers games from Ebbets Field; and Vin Scully, the golden voice of the World Series every October. Every Memorial Day, we listened in the backyard to the announcers anchored around the turns at the Indianapolis 500, "The Greatest Spectacle in Racing," a cascade of thrilling sounds that we converted into pictures in our mind's eye. Most evenings, my parents listened to the news in the dining room, and I listened intensely to the deep baritone of Edward R. Morrow, whose tone exuded authority. His sign off, "Good night, and good luck," blessed many of our dinner hours. On weekdays, Mother listened to the Canadian stations from Toronto and Hamilton, Ontario, that featured classical music introduced by announcers. Their ability to pronounce composers' names like Modest Mussorgsky, Igor Stravinsky, Jacques Ibert, and Georg Philipp Telemann, and to say Wolfgang Amadeus Mozart and Johann Sebastian Bach with a distinctly Germanic accent convinced me that Canadians were smarter than most of our neighbors on Highgate. My life-long love of classical music began in the broadcasts that transformed Mother's crowded kitchen into a grand concert hall every afternoon.

Because I associated particular voices with the words they spoke—Mel Allen pontificating on another Mickey Mantle home run or a Canadian announcer introducing a Bach concerto—I realized that how one spoke mattered nearly as much as what one said, and this association launched my love of the spoken word. For thirty-three years, working as an English professor and immersed in literature that Mother taught me to love, I told my students that they had to read literature out loud; they had to *hear* Hamlet or Othello, *hear* the musical prose of Scott Fitzgerald, *hear* the crisp dialogue spoken by immigrant Jews in Grace Paley's Greenwich Village. Like blood, words should flow through the body, driven by the accents of a distinct human voice. Every poetry reading or concert I attend today seems to emanate from that Philco radio in the dining room or Mother's small one in the kitchen.

When Father plunked a small, black-and-white television into the living room in 1953, our family's entertainment habits altered and not necessarily for the better. We watched more and listened less. The television introduced TV din-ners eaten off plastic plates on flimsy, stackable, metal tables arranged so that we watched while we ate. This rearrangement of the dinner hour decreased the often-lively conversation that punctuated our evening meals, and although we did not camp in front of the television every night, when we did, something vital was lost. The programs in the mid-1950s were "wholesome" or "family oriented," and many were hilarious: *I Love Lucy*, *Jack Benny*, *The Honeymooners* with Jackie Gleason and Art Carney, and *Show of Shows* with Sid Caesar, Imogene Cocoa, and Carl Reiner. I watched rather than listened to baseball games, and when I saw the faces of Red Barber or Vin Scully, I was shocked to realize how wrong my imag-ined pictures of them had been: Barber was too old and Scully too skinny. Their voices, with their distinct rhythms that were part of the game itself and painted verbal pictures, remained inviolate. The voices of my childhood, even from my earliest years, remain more prominent in my memory than the pictures. Today, in our Seattle home, there are radios everywhere—living room, study, kitchen, bedroom, workshop, studio—and the television languishes in the cellar.

For much of my childhood, the house was overrun with animals, a fact of life on Highgate that Mother loved and Father endured. Brandy, my black Lab, shared living quarters with several species: a small black dog that Aunt Kay owned that had serious bladder and bowel problems (with expected results in the house) and that Father threatened to kill, several cats, a large black-and-white rabbit named Thumper that was hit by a car and suffered a broken leg for which Father fashioned a wooden splint, the two ducks that competed with Father for his Saturday-night bath, mice, two or three at a time, that Mary Lee kept in small cardboard boxes, and several parakeets. My parents argued frequently and loudly about these residents.

"Mary, why the hell do we need another animal in this house?"
"Well, the kids like pets, and I thought having rabbits would be fun. I thought they could stay in the backyard all summer."
"You thought! You never think of asking me what I think about this! Where are they going to stay in the winter?"
"Well, they can stay in the basement with the dogs and the cats, or Mandy and Anne can keep them in their bedroom."

Substitute ducks, mice, parakeets, Aunt Kay's mutt, a stray cat—the picture crystallizes.

The rationale—if there was one—for the location of the parakeet cage was never clear. Mother and Mary Lee suspended it from a metal bracket that they screwed into an oak pillar at the far end of the dining room above the place where Father sat during dinner. The chain from the bracket to the top of the cage was a bit long, and when Father sat down for dinner, his head was precariously close to the bottom of the cage. Innumerable times, forgetting the location of the cage, he sat up abruptly and smacked his head on it. Wham! Chaos! The cage swung wildly on its chain, terrifying the birds that screeched as if under attack, Father raged about the "goddamn birds and all the other lousy animals in this house," Mother tried to calm him while simultaneously trying not to laugh, and we kids thought the scene hysterical. When for the umpteenth time Father asked

Mother why the cage was hung over his chair, she mumbled about the parakeets not wanting to be lonely at dinner. Father railed at us, "And just what do you think is so damn funny?" and cursed his way into the kitchen where he slammed his dishes and descended into his workshop in the basement, never to return that night. Around the table we exploded in laughter at the poor man who suffered mightily in what he thought was *his* home.

Besides my bedroom, a space that I treasured was what we called the sitting room. This was a small section at the front of the living room that faced the street and was secluded by narrow walls and two beautiful, floor-to-ceiling glass doors. During the winter, after satisfying Mother's conviction that playing outside built strong character, we dashed straight for the sitting room and its comfy couch, cuddling cups of hot chocolate while gazing at the swirling whiteness that we left behind. (Mother adored winter storms and was convinced that her children should learn to take advantage of them. Why waste a howling blizzard and minus-fifteen-degree wind chill? Consider what playing outside in such weather for two hours could *do* for you!) For years, in this room-within-a-room, we erected our Christmas tree, and its lights blazed through the windows and illuminated the eternal snow on the front lawn. On Christmas Eve, my parents left the tree lights burning all night so that, they said, Santa Claus could find our house. Before going to bed, I went outside, stood on the lawn, and gazed at the shining lights that festooned the tree. Before my father for some inexplicable reason razed the walls and removed the doors, I often retreated to this alcove, closed the doors, and read for hours on the big couch that stretched below the front windows. Late at night, it became another room that I called my own, and I was immensely saddened when Father destroyed it, probably to create a larger living room. I still cherish small, cozy rooms that offer seclusion. They are like another womb where I can almost defy time.

Such was the house on Highgate. It was chaotic, noisy, rambunctious, magical, full of people, pets, and (I still believe) little Irish visitors. Within its rooms, my parents maintained and nourished their family as best they could under difficult circumstances. No parents ever completely succeed in the terrifying responsibility of raising children, nor can one define what constitutes "successful" parenting. Appreciating the consequences for one's later life demands not only remembering where one began but also understanding how the personalities of one's parents influenced how and what they taught their children.

CHAPTER 2:
WILLIAM AND MARY

In a seventh grade writing assignment for Sister Roseanne at Saint Aloysius Gonzaga School, I proudly proclaimed, "On June 20, 1943 my mother presented my father with his first real prob-lem: me." That's precocious for a seventh grader, but when I con-sider my parents' married life, I think it was prescient. Opposites attract, but in temperament, dis-position, and interests, my par-ents were amazingly different people. Mother was energetic, loquacious, and gregarious; Father calculating, taciturn, and reserved. Mother told me a story about coming home with Father from a party where they met some of his colleagues. When Father asked her how she liked them, she said, "Well, they're nice people, but they're awfully quiet." He said, "There's nothing wrong with quiet people!" He remarked

WILLIAM & MARY; JUNE 20, 1942

that if she died first, he would inscribe on her tomb, "She detested peace and quiet." No married man ever sought so fervently the quiet that he never found.

My parents' personal differences mirrored their disparate origins. Father was born in Kiev, Ukraine, in 1910 to an Austrian father, Daniel Otto Sczurgot (born 1878), and a Polish mother, Catherine Kwasnycia (born 1887). Father emigrated with his parents and siblings, Frank and Stella, from Bremen, Germany, in either 1913 or 1914, depending on either his mother's oft-repeated family history (1914) or the records from Ellis Island (1913), where the original spelling was changed to Shurgot. Father's sister, Olga, and brothers, Lee and Daniel, were born in Buffalo. Mother's ancestors were Irish and German, but as the joke about Paddy and Mike indicates, her Irish heritage dominated her life and hence her children's. Her Irish grandparents, Edward Charles Brown, born in Dublin, and Julia O'Hollaran from County Clare, immigrated to the United States in the 1880s and married in Buffalo. Among their eleven children (two of whom died in infancy) was Helen Brown, my mother's mother. On July 13, 1907, Helen Brown married John Joseph Spitzig, a tall, distinguished German whom I called "J. J." and who moved to Buffalo from Walkerton, Ontario. John and Helen had three daughters, all born in Buffalo: Loraine in 1910, Mother in 1914, and Catherine in 1916. I draw my ethnic heritage from disparate and often warring European nations, and although the relatives of my extended family tolerated each other, I suspect that my grandmother never forgave her son William for not marrying a nice, quiet Polish girl.

In her tortured memoir, *Drinking: A Love Story*, Caroline Knapp wrote the saddest sentence I have ever read: "Growing up, I never heard my parents say 'I love you,' not to us and not to each other." That is incomprehensible to me. Although from a man my age that assertion seems sentimental and suggests naïveté about parents' emotional reticence in older generations, it is nonetheless true. My parents' ethnic histories were wildly different, and perhaps at times the motivations for their words or actions were opaque, but neither I nor my sisters doubted that they loved each other.

One of my most cherished photos was taken in the dining room on Highgate in the early Sixties. Father is wearing a plaid wool shirt and corduroy pants, and Mother is wearing an apron over her skirt and sweater. Father is standing next to the large oak table, and Mother is leaning her right forearm on a chair next to the table, her left hand resting upon her hip. They are kissing. The striking feature of this photo is its casualness: an informal romantic moment, two people married about twenty years, expressing mutual love in the midst of their daily routine, perhaps something as mundane as clearing the table. Someone, Aunt Kay perhaps, snapped them stealing a kiss, as if they had met by chance at the corner of the table. I marvel at Mother's resting her arm upon the chair, suggesting a nonchalance that belies their marital history. Oh, that I could find that photo!

Mother graduated from Mount Saint Joseph Academy and worked at various office jobs. Father, a superb athlete, aspired to be a physical education teacher, and I believe he would have been an excellent instructor. However, after completing his studies at Indiana Normal College, now Indiana State University, he returned to Buffalo and began a career in business. He worked as a purchasing agent for several industries, many of which, including General Electric, Frederick Flater, and Sterling Engine, held military contracts during World War II and the Cold War. I suspect that Father was disappointed about not pursuing a career in education, but had he done so, he never would have met Mother. They met in late 1941 while they were both working at Goodyear, and they married on June 20, 1942. My birthday, exactly one year later, was not only their anniversary but also Father's Day. Thereafter, they believed that Father's Day occurring on June 20 was auspicious.

My parents assumed the traditional roles for married couples in the 1940s and 1950s. Father worked full time, and for the remainder of her married life Mother was a homemaker. There was nothing unusual or remarkable about these roles, and although I am sure that neither desired a different arrangement, I marvel that, at least outwardly, my relentlessly energetic mother never chafed at this arrangement. Because Father worked primarily for industries that survived on military contracts, especially during the Cold War, he could be unemployed for months when his company failed to secure military orders. He was too proud to admit that at times he failed as a provider, and even though the extra income would have been welcomed, Mother chose not to worsen the situation by working outside the home.

My parents were not "sophisticated people." They did not frequent formal dinner parties or the opera. Their "foreign travel" was limited to Ontario and Quebec, Canada. They seldom attended the Buffalo Philharmonic, never attended live theatre, and saw movies only occasionally. They drank beer, not wine, with dinner (Ballantine Ale and/or Pabst Blue Ribbon) and did not belong to a private golf or country club. They once had a new car (1964 Chevy II) but usually drove battered beaters that my Uncle Frank miraculously kept running. Although we periodically visited the Polish markets on Pederewski Street where Mother bought Polish sausage and kielbasa, and she regularly patronized the German specialty shops on Bailey Avenue, much of our food came from the Nu-Way Supermarket and consisted of the typical American diet: meat or poultry with mashed potatoes drenched in margarine or French fries doused in ketchup, fried fish every Friday, mostly canned but some fresh fruits and vegetables, Campbell's soup, and bushel baskets of peanut-butter-and-jelly sandwiches served on Wonder Bread that could be mashed into the corners of a lunch pail. If PB & J on Wonder Bread were lethal, I would have died sixty years ago. The margarine that Mother used during World War II was the strangest substance I have ever seen. When Father was unemployed, we often obtained rations at an armory on Delavan Avenue. Among these rations was a plastic bag filled with a yellow substance, probably vegetable oils and God knows what else, in the middle of which sat a red dot. Father kneaded this bag on the kitchen table until the red dot disappeared, and then, so the directions claimed, one had "margarine." Right! Watching the dot gradually disappear was fascinating, but as a parent who fed his growing children organic everything, I shudder to think what was in that plastic container. Only on Thanksgiving, Christmas, and Easter would we get special seasonal meals: turkey at Thanksgiving and Christmas and ham at Easter with all the trimmings, including Mother's delicious pies.

There was always enough to eat, but I realized later how severely limited my family diet had been. At a reception in Minneapolis at the Guthrie Theatre in 1966, I spread on a cracker a large dollop of what I thought was blackberry jam. In the midst of this sophisticated crowd, I bit into the cracker, and my gut revolted! As I reached for a handkerchief, I heard someone behind me praise the excellent caviar. I had no damn idea what that word meant and haven't touched the stuff since. I was equally perplexed the first time I saw the word *yogurt* on a menu at Al's Breakfast in Dinky Town, the favorite café of students at the University of Minnesota. Confusing yogurt with yurt, I thought that perhaps yogurt meant a structure where hippies went to meditate. I did not ponder why a canvas tent would be on a breakfast menu. Baffled, I asked the girl next to me what yogurt was, and she glared at me as if I were from a distant planet. Well, no, I was from my parents' house on Highgate.

My parents' tastes were incompatible. Despite having only a high school education, Mother read constantly. The small bookshelf in our living room contained numerous editions of *Reader's Digest Condensed Books* and a paperback selection of American poets, where I discovered Robert Frost's early poems, "Mending Wall," "Birches," and "After Apple Picking" ("But I am done with apple-picking now. / Essence of winter sleep is on the night"). There was an anthology of Irish literature, including works by James Stephens, Liam O' Flaherty, James Joyce,

Sean O'Casey, and Mother's favorite, W. B. Yeats. Thomas's "A Child's Christmas in Wales" profoundly influenced my young imagination. Mother also cherished classical music from her Canadian station and the broadcasts of the Metropolitan Opera from New York City. Father had little use for literature or music. When Mother listened to the opera on Saturday afternoons, he paraded around the house parodying with guttural clamor whatever famous tenor was belting out Puccini, Mozart, or Wagner.

My parents' favorite entertainment was inviting relatives or friends to the house for a Saturday evening dinner and card games. The dinners, especially on summer evenings with Father's brothers, Lee and Frank, and their families, were loud, unruly gatherings of the clan that spilled into the back yard and thoroughly annoyed the neighbors, especially those who went to bed before midnight. Frank's voice trumpeted over the tumult, especially once he, Lee, and Father downed several shots and matching beers and wandered outside to continue whatever argument they had begun during dinner. On long winter nights, my parents invited people to the house for drinks and card games that turned the dining room into a veritable saloon. Many nights I wandered downstairs to pee well past midnight and walked through a haze of cigarette smoke and past stacks of beer bottles. I lay awake hearing shouts of triumph and, especially if my uncles were in the game, constant cussing from the games of bridge or pinochle that exploded below.

Father devoted his energies to his work while Mother poured hers into pleasing her husband and raising children. She believed, for example, that because her husband worked hard at the office, his daily homecoming should be worthy of the family's attention. She ensured that we were "spiffed up" for his arrival: hair combed, clothes changed, and ribbons in my sisters' hair. After he parked the car in the driveway, we lined up at the head of the steps leading to the side door, and each of us greeted him and opened our arms for a kiss and a hug. He responded gratefully but was often less effusive than we expected. Although we never faulted him, at least not openly, we often sensed impatience, as if all he wanted was to collapse into his chair by the fireplace and read the evening paper. Spending time with children, especially, sadly, his daughters, was not exactly an annoyance but rather something that he believed was primarily a mother's responsibility. In this regard, he was not unique for his generation. Fathers generated, mothers nurtured. I know nothing about my father's early childhood in Ukraine or his youth in Buffalo, and I never knew his father (who left the family and died in Los Angeles in 1950). I suspect, however, that the "Old World" paternal hierarchy pertained throughout Father's childhood and that, as a parent, he replicated what he experienced as a child.

Father could neither understand nor subdue Mother's energy. She wanted to pack every day with activities, while he preferred to rest, especially whenever she believed that the whole family should "do something together" regardless of the season or the condition of our rattling automobiles. In the summer, "doing something together" meant organizing picnics and, to his consternation, inviting several neighborhood kids, including Danny Miller, whose parents never took him anywhere, and the three Dressel brothers, whose parents seldom had a working car. Summers meant driving across the Peace Bridge to Sherkston Beaches, Ontario, where Lake Erie was supposedly cleaner than the Buffalo side, portions of which had been turned into orange sludge by several industries, especially the giant steel plant in Lackawanna. Never mind the cars crawling across the steaming bridge carrying sweaty kids and cranky parents to the same crowded Canadian beaches. An equally appealing Canadian destination was Crystal Beach, an amusement park filled with acres of thrilling rides. The most famous and dangerous was The Comet, a second cousin to an earlier roller coaster called The Cyclone, which was so treacherous that a nurse was on duty at the end of the ride to aid sickened riders. Each time we rode The Comet, we bet on which kid would vomit last before the ride ended. I always lost.

Autumn meant long drives to Letchworth State Park to see the changing colors and the mammoth railroad trestle that loomed eighty feet above the gorge. When Mother proposed this annual trek in early October, Father said, "Well Mary, we went there last fall," but she assured him that the children would enjoy going again. After all, the beautiful fall colors might be different from last year's and thus must be seen. Here Mary Lee walked along the narrow stone wall above the gorge, starting at the sign that read "Danger: Keep Off" and terrified Mother. Winter necessitated equally long drives to Chestnut Ridge Park, south of Buffalo near Orchard Park, to go tobogganing, a sport that we children loved because of the death-defying thrill rides down the icy slopes to the bottom of the run where we always "crashed" just before the row of trees at the end. Father disliked tobogganing because he had to lug the toboggan back up the hill after our rides. Our other winter destination was Ellicott Creek Park off Niagara Falls Boulevard, where we skated on the frozen pond. Father, the only non-skater in the family, sat patiently inside the warming house with a thermos of hot chocolate waiting for us to exhaust ourselves or fall and twist an ankle. On all such excursions, Mother exclaimed, "Isn't this fun!" thus assuring that another perfectly good (i.e., cold) winter day was not wasted. Father replied, "Whatever you say, Hon" and mumbled about chores he should be doing at home or a football game he could be watching.

Father's married life would have been less challenging had he been more assertive. Consider parades, one of Mother's favorite activities. Every year we attended both the Saint Patrick's and Christmas parades. The weather for both was often miserable: a cold rain for Saint Patrick's and a snowstorm for Christmas. Mother believed that the weather must never be a deterrent to attending either parade; in fact, braving the weather was part of the "joy" of the experience. Whether Father or we children wanted to attend the parade was irrelevant, and we were not consulted. She wrapped us in layers of wool sweaters, scarves, boots, gloves, and heavy coats and bundled us into the car. Father drove downtown, dropped us off somewhere near the parade route, and spent forty minutes finding a parking space. When he eventually found us, Mother asked him, "What took you so long?" as if the poor man had been looking for parking on Mars. We stood for three hours, enduring the miserable weather and watching numerous Irish marching bands play the same tunes over and over, or gazed longingly at school children costumed as Santa's elfin helpers while choral groups and high school bands played familiar carols. Mother insisted that we stay until the end of each parade because if we left early, we missed something. We especially could not leave the Christmas parade early, because at the end, Santa rode by in his sled, and we came to see *him!* Mother shouted "Oh look," at every passing Irish band or wailing carolers, while Father remarked quietly that we had seen and heard the same groups for years.

Many years later during a family gathering in Canton, Ohio, she reminded him about the many parades we had seen during all those years in Buffalo.

"Weren't those parades fun, honey?"

"Mary," he said flatly, "I hated parades."

"What?" she asked incredulously. "Why didn't you say something then?"

"Mary, it wouldn't have done any good. I would have had to go anyway."

He was right. Protests against attending parades would have been futile. Had he ever resisted, she would have taken us herself and created in Father a sense of guilt that he never could have expunged and that she never would have let him forget. Parades existed to be watched; if people worked to stage them, we were obligated to attend them. Father's fondest wish during these parades was to retreat into one of the many bars along Delaware Avenue to down a few beers and get warm, and on parade days, he envied the guys who enjoyed the festivities from inside one of these fine establishments. Pity the married man out in the cold pretending that he enjoyed parades!

To understand how long-suffering his married life was, one must also understand Mother's unlimited capacity for imagined deprivation. Because she never wanted to miss anything, if any planned activity—even a day's drive somewhere out of town—went awry, she pouted, played the martyr, and made him feel responsible for her pain. A missed day at the beach was catastrophic. She acted as if she were the only mother of three in Buffalo who was deprived of an escape from a sweltering August day. To expound on her suffering she evoked her favorite paradigm: the end of the world.

> "Holy Jesus, but it's hot, and this might have been our last chance to go to the beach all summer. Now how will we get through the rest of the summer? It's only August 14! Never mind next weekend; the car will probably have to go in again for repairs, and by then it will be almost September and then it's too chilly to enjoy the beach. And Labor Day weekend it's so crowded on the Peace Bridge there's no point in even trying to get across, and even if you could, the beaches are always so packed there's no place to park the car or spread out a blanket. You'd practically have to get up at three a.m."

And so on. Father did not dare go near her, and we kids sulked around the house, afraid to suggest another activity for fear of setting off an explosion of grief about the missed opportunity that would *never* return!

In Conor McPherson's play, *The Seafarer,* the blind drunk, Richard, fearing that his brother Sharky will refuse to give him a "Jaysus fucking drink" on Christmas Eve and so "blow the whole Christmas atmosphere," complains to Sharky, "This is all I have! And how many do I have left? Maybe only this one! Maybe that's it for me!" When Sharky asks him, "What are you talking about?" Richard responds, "Ah! It's hardly even worth it! What's the point?" A brilliantly Irish existential plunge from the trivial to the tragic! From a missed drink (or day at the beach) to musings about the whole purpose of our dismal, shabby existence. In McPherson's play, Richard never stops to think that maybe if he quit drinking he might experience several more holidays, and Mother could not imagine another plan for a day that had not gone as expected. Like Richard, she was damn sure that everyone else in the house had to suffer accordingly.

Despite my parents' starkly different personalities, they thoroughly enjoyed and enthusiastically celebrated Christmas. Even when Father had been out of work or his income had dimin-ished, my parents insisted on a festive holiday celebration. Christmas included several tradi-tions that endured from year to year yet because of my parents' enthusiasm for the season never seemed boring. Mother insisted on getting a real tree, and on Christmas Eve, we decorated it with tinsel, ornaments, glass bulbs, and strings of multicol-ored lights. Some lights always failed to work, sending Father into the cold to a hardware store looking for replacements.

MY PARENTS, GAIL AND I, MARA AND NICHO-LAS; CHRISTMAS, 1974; CANTON, OHIO

Mother played repeatedly "The Holly and the Ivy" by the Mormon Tabernacle Choir and the Christmas albums that I purchased at the Goodyear Service Station. She made eggnog and, like Auntie Hanna in Thomas's "A Child's Christmas in Wales," laced it with rum, and as we decorated the tree, even the children got a spirited nog.

Midnight Mass was required, and at Saint Aloysius, it lasted ninety min-utes. Because the church was crowded with what Mother called "one timers" who attended Mass only on Christmas Eve, we arrived at 11:00 p.m. to get a seat near the front. The church was splendidly decorated. Poinsettias bloomed everywhere, huge wreaths and sprigs of holly tied with red bows hung on every pillar, potent incense enveloped us, and six tall candles burning on the main altar lighted our way out of the long, cold darkness. Carols sung from the choir loft filled the church and evoked the sensuous beauty and mystery of this holy night. While other children chatted with friends and showed off their holiday apparel,

I sat quietly, awaiting the chimes that announced the first minutes of Christmas and heralded the solemn service: the priest's white and gold vestments, his ritualized gestures, the Latin prayers, the incense, the communion service with the transfigured bread and wine, and the priest's blessings from the high altar that together transformed all the world. In seventh and eighth grade, as an altar boy, I served High Mass or sang in the boys' choir. The sense of participating in solemn rituals became immensely powerful, and it remains one of the most compelling memories of my childhood.

Christmas also meant setting up the Lionel model train. Even as a young child I was fascinated by trains. Whenever my grandfather, J. J. Spitzig, who worked for the Pennsylvania Railroad, visited our house on Sunday afternoons, we sat in the backyard listening for the thundering steam engines in the Pennsylvania freight yards up at the corner of Main Street and Hurdle Avenue. Grandpa J. J. claimed that he heard the engines, and I, of course, agreed. We jumped into his Ford and drove up Highgate to the yard where we pulled into the gravel road next to the tracks and watched the iron beasts shuffle freight cars back and forth. Santa Claus must have heard about these visits, because for Christmas 1947, he delivered a Lionel 027-gauge Pennsylvania 6-8-6 turbine

Mary Lee, Anne and I with Mother and cat; Christmas, 2000; Buffalo

steam engine with four freight cars and a bright-red caboose. (I still have that engine, and it still runs!) Every Christmas thereafter he carried in his sleigh many of the orange and white cartons, each with distinct blue lettering across the top in block letters: LIONEL ELECTRIC TRAINS.

Starting in 1948, setting up the model train became a ritual in itself. Shortly after Thanksgiving, I began pestering Father after dinner about when we were going to start. I stood at his right elbow and implored, "Tonight, Dad?" We began by going into the attic with flashlights and digging out the large cardboard boxes in which we stored the train equipment. I gingerly opened each of the Lionel cartons and inspected its contents. As I acquired more freight and passenger cars, I sometimes marveled at finding a tank car or boxcar that I had forgotten I owned, and so each November, plunging into these orange and white cartons was a joyous rediscovery of miniature treasures. I lined up the cars and cleaned them and lubricated the engines to ensure that they ran efficiently. Father reassembled the table, either in the basement or in the attic, and then we planned the layout. I always hoped that another Christmas would yield more engines and more rolling stock and thus the capacity to enlarge this treasured, imaginary world we re-created every December. While I dreaded the spring day that Father would disassemble the train, taking it down always created anticipation for setting it up again the following winter. I realize now that this annual winter-to-spring-to-winter cycle contributed to my developing sense that we must honor each season with its appropriate rituals, for these are the markers of our lives.

The other memorable event was our family's annual excursion to Muskoka, a name still enchanting in my memory. The Muskoka Lakes of central Ontario nestled amid dense forests dotted by resorts, lodges, and cabins that catered to American and Canadian families seeking a rustic retreat. From the late Forties to the late Fifties, when Father was gainfully employed and had a two-week vacation, we spent one full week in a cabin on Mortimer's Point. We vacationed in late August after enduring three sweaty months of Buffalo's steamy, polluted summer. Anticipation commenced in early August, when my sisters and I pestered our parents about when we would leave. We packed and unpacked several times, all the while badgering Father about how much room we would have in the car for our "stuff." Regardless of what he said, the night before the trip we deposited at Father's feet suitcases crammed with clothes, toys, dolls, food, thermoses, maps, shoes, slippers, and blankets ("It gets cold up there at night"; "Mary, there will be blankets at the cabin") that he vainly tried to cram into the trunk. I imagined Hannibal trying to load one more sack of armor on that last, beleaguered elephant before heading across the Alps. Father complained about the sheer volume of what Mother insisted that we needed for just one week, just as he did about having to stand around watching parades, but to no avail. The Canadian immigration officer checking our trunk at the Rainbow Bridge in Lewiston probably thought that we planned to stay for two months.

Father woke us at five o'clock. We tried to get an early start, failed, and thus got stuck in major traffic jams heading north into Ontario's vacation lands. The drive took eight to ten torturous hours, the car was not air conditioned, and the three kids were crabby from lack of sleep. We never ceased asking Father when we would get there, beginning just after we crossed into Ontario. Both my parents smoked the entire way. One hour after entering Canada, Mother recalled some essential item she forgot that she insisted we had to go back for, and hours later, oblivious to the crowded highway and Father's increasing frustration, she wondered aloud why the journey was taking so long. Nonetheless, this great adventure of our childhood was exhilarating. We headed north on Queen Elizabeth Way through St. Catharine, to Hamilton along the shores of Lake Ontario, and then northeast to Mississauga and York. We then went north again on Highway 400 through Richmond Hill and Newmarket and Barrie on Lake Simcoe, where we turned northeast on Highway 11 and drove through Orilla to Severn Bridge, Gravenhurst, and Bracebridge. Driving west on Highway 118 to Port Carling, the last town on our journey, we finally arrived on the dirt road that led to the main lodge at Lake Muskoka.

We entered an exotic wilderness of huge trees; gleaming lakes and flowing rivers; abundant wildlife, including deer, raccoons, beavers, bear, elk, coyotes, and probably wolves; and millions of birds, including eagles. Our cabin was a beautiful, secluded retreat nestled among pines and firs and offered gorgeous views of the lake, especially at sunset. The rooms featured knotty-pine paneling and furniture. We slept in bunk beds, and every night we had a roaring fire. Tucked into the main lodge was a tiny shop that sold Silverton Ice Cream, the best I have ever tasted, until ten o'clock and was our last stop before walking back to our cabin. In Port Carling and Bracebridge, we found small shops with the skins of deer, bear, and beaver tacked onto the walls. The shops sold Indian moccasins, dresses, and beads that we begged our parents to buy for us.

We were called to breakfast at seven o'clock by a huge bell atop the main lodge that resounded throughout the woods, summoning us to the most idyllic days of our childhood. We climbed Mount Baldy and planted a small flag cut from a sheet on which we wrote the family name and drew an imagined family crest. We walked around the edge of the lake to a beach with pure white sand and dove off "the rock" into the cleanest water I had ever seen. Father rowed us around the lake in a beautifully finished rowboat while displaying the muscular physique that Mother loved to watch in motion. We rode ferryboats from Port Carling to distant lakes connected by a system of locks that completely baffled Mother and that Father tried to explain. We hiked into the forest behind our cabin along what I believed was an endless trail. I often imagined walking it forever so that I would not have to return to Buffalo. Such was the allure of this Canadian retreat that passed as wilderness and provided a cherished peace for all our family.

After dinner, we played shuffleboard or Father rowed us a short way onto the lake to experience its lingering calm. Later, we sat on the cabin porch and watched evening descend over the hushed forest as the dazzling light of a billion stars danced across the sky. Mother and Father relaxed, sibling rivalries disappeared, and we experienced a tranquility that we seldom knew in Buffalo. Here too during every visit, as at Midnight Mass each Christmas, a sense of renewal swept through me. I believed that despite the tensions that I increasingly realized existed within our family, life for us would be wholesome and rewarding, peaceful and plentiful. The dancing stars on those endlessly beautiful nights promised us.

Every kid remembers a time when one of the essential scenes of childhood, if not childhood itself, ended. Such a moment occurred one sultry August evening in 1959 when my parents announced that we were not going to Muskoka that summer. It was a hammer blow that I can still feel. Father had been out of work, and there was no money for a vacation anywhere, much less Muskoka. We would not be making that long, arduous, but ultimately renewing journey north to the knotty-pine castle in the wilderness. No trees, rivers, lakes, swimming, Silverton Ice Cream, howling coyotes (if not wolves), shuffleboard, ferry rides, sunsets, stars, or family crest on Mount Baldy. Nothing! We had driven out that dirt road, out of that enchanted forest, for the last time. The rhythm of my childhood was irreparably broken; an essential cog in the wheel of time by which I measured the seasons of my life was sheared. Never again would I gaze into a winter night from my bedroom window and remember that summer's final walk on the endless path into the Muskoka woods and believe that next August I would venture even farther into its forbidding depths. Without that annual bucolic retreat that formed an essential part of every year, nothing seemed secure.

There were other family excursions, including trips to Aunt Loraine's cabin at Timber Top, a cabin owned by Margaret O'Brien, a high school friend of Mother's, in the Boston Hills outside Buffalo, and a trip to Washington, DC, to visit former Highgate neighbors. A vacation in Michigan produced one of our family's most bizarre journeys. At a goodbye party that my parents hosted for one of Father's best friends, Gene McEvoy ("Mack"), he invited us to visit him in Michigan. Six sheets to the wind, he drew on the back of our kitchen door his proposed sleeping arrangements. Father left the drawings intact, and when the following summer he decided to visit the McEvoys, he removed the kitchen door, cut out the central panel, strapped it to a makeshift carrier on top of the Chevy, and hauled it all the way to Michigan. We were nutty Buffalo vagabonds driving along highways with a door panel strapped to the top of the car! When we pulled into Mack's driveway, he damn near died laughing. As a tribute to that adventure, Father never painted over Mack's drawing. I gleefully recall that trip, and I wish that Father had exhibited more often the freewheeling spirit that he engineered for that trek to Michigan. These escapes from Buffalo brought a measure of joy to the family, and my sisters and I always appreciated our parents' efforts, but no other destination ever rivaled Muskoka during the most enjoyable and impressionable years of my childhood.

Besides these actual journeys, there were many imagined ones. On summer nights, Father often drove the family toward the airport. He parked the car along Cleveland Drive under the flight path for departing planes, and as we watched them leaving Buffalo, we tried to guess their destination.

"Maybe that big jet is going to Chicago, or maybe New York or even San Francisco."
"It might even be going to London or Paris."
"Mom, can we take a plane somewhere sometime?"
"Well, maybe someday. We'll see."

We never did, but all the way home, we conjured exotic journeys to distant lands.

What to make of the above? My parents were starkly different people. Mother detested peace and quiet and irrepressibly sought adventure; Father patiently endured innumerable parades and outings while craving rest and reprieve from parenting. Despite their differences and mutual embrace of traditional and clearly delineated parenting roles, each endeavored to provide a loving and stimulating home for their children. They tolerated their differences, seldom raised their voices to one another or to their children, persevered through iceboxes and coal bins, unemployment and beat-up cars, sent their kids to excellent schools, provided them with a modicum of material goods, and were totally devoted to one another.

My father died of pancreatic cancer in Canton, Ohio, on August 28, 1975, the day my family arrived in El Paso where I began my teaching career at the University of Texas-El Paso. (He never saw my name on my office door; piss on the gods for that!) Two days later, I flew back to Canton for his funeral at which, oddly, neither I nor anyone else gave a eulogy. I arrived the night before the funeral, and Mother and I talked for several hours. She told me that during my father's final weeks, he was so weak that he could not bathe himself, and so she washed him. She sat Father in the bathtub and, God love her Irish humor, told him that he was receiving the services of "Holy Mary's Scald Your Balls Bath Service." Mother refused to believe that Father would not survive his cancer, and perhaps she thought that hot water and humor would soothe her husband's soul, if not his dying body.

She said to me, "Your father and I were together the night before he died." How astonishing! The night before my wasted father died, he and his wife of thirty-three years were "together." Maybe all she meant was that they had cuddled on the couch downstairs, or perhaps Father had been able to mount the stairs to their bedroom, and they had held each other for the last time in their bed. Maybe they made love; maybe they loved each other physically as they had come to understand that word during my father's long illness. I don't know, and the exact meaning of her use of "together" does not matter. I have no reason to doubt her stories about either the bathing or the loving. As the Irish refrain asks, "And who's to say it isn't true?"

At a dinner party in Seattle in May 2009, I told a psychologist that I was writing a memoir, and he asked me, "What myths are you pursuing in your memoir?" The Greek *mythos* means simply "story," even though it has come to mean "something that is not true." A memoir recounts stories about what has been and continues to be most vital in our lives and our families, for these stories sustain us through time and generations. Those stories are always true. One of the stories I tell here is about my parents as genuinely loving people who *never* ceased caring for each other—recall the casual kiss at the dining room table—and who taught their children that loving one another is the only gift worth giving.

CHAPTER 3:
PARENTS AND SIBLINGS

—⚊—

Mother was the dominant parent in her children's lives. Having accepted the traditional roles of wife and mother, and having had her first child on her first wedding anniversary, she channeled her enthusiasm and energy into nurturing her children. Father worked hard, provided for his family, and expected deference and loyalty from his wife and obedience and respect from his children. He was astonishingly shy and emotionally lean. Except for a practicality in Anne, a knack for tools and love of sports in Mary Lee, and my love of baseball and model trains, we three children are temperamentally far more our mother's children than our father's. Her warmth, openness, love of stories, gaiety, and sheer zest for life's possibilities permeate her children's lives.

WILLIAM & MARY, MICHAEL, ANNE, MARY LEE; BUFFALO, 1952

Most men probably have no idea what to expect when they marry and wake up one morning dumbfounded by the responsibilities of fatherhood. I am certain that at times Father not only wished for the quiet, ordered life he led before he married but also barely tolerated the household that he and Mother created. She was not a quiet person. Her concept of parenting always involved "doing something with the kids" or "taking them somewhere" *together*; that word was the key to her vision of family life. Given her enormous energy and eternal optimism, she believed that the more time she and Father spent engaged with their children, the more curious and creative they would become. Conversely, he seemed at times annoyed by the demands of his children, as if we were all a burden, an afterthought in his marriage. One can perhaps explain Father's occasional indifference to them in many ways: Old World views of parental responsibilities, the mystery of why any two people marry, the emotional complexity at the heart of any one human being, the personalities of children as they develop within a family, and how those developing children relate to their parents as they grow and their parents age. More likely, all of the above. To readers of my generation, there may be little mystery to my parents' parenting, but as I wander through my memories of where I started and how all that molded whom I have become as a son, husband, and father, some sifting of this issue remains to be done.

I realize now that Mother was often disappointed, even angered, by Father's diffidence toward his children, especially Mary Lee and Anne. During a visit to El Paso in October 1976, a year after Father died, she said to me, "Your father was a wonderful husband but a lousy father." Given what I saw and remember of their relationship, I have no reason to doubt the former statement, but despite what I have said above about family togetherness, Christmas, Muskoka, etc., and the singular need for familial love, I admit that there is truth in the latter. These sketches evoke primarily a joyous romp through a jumble of warring uncles, skittish aunts, a bustling neighborhood of friends and endless street games, paper routes, dogs, cats, rabbits, ducks, snow, more snow, and excursions enough to fill all four seasons. Memory is, as Richard White cogently observes, "the shifting record of the sense we make of things." Memory shifts because we age, because it is selective and protects us from what we either pretend never happened or refuse to acknowledge. Every child in every family experiences childhood differently, even in those fortunate families where the parents remain together, are civil toward one another, and care deeply for their children. The sense I am trying to make of the childhood I shared with Mary Lee and Anne is different from their sense of living with the same parents in the same house on Highgate. As the oldest child and the only male in my mother's extended family, I was adored by Grandpa J. J., who was thrilled to have a grandson. Uncle Frank had one son, Uncle Lee had two daughters, Father's sisters, Olga and Stella, were childless, and Father's youngest brother, Daniel Jr., never married. Given that Mother's sisters were also childless, I was coveted by aunts and uncles who constantly asked me about school and told me that they expected much of me. By age five or six, I felt deeply obligated to relatives who admonished me to obey my parents and to study hard.

Despite my perception of our parents' strikingly different relationships with their children, I believe that my sisters would agree that despite our parents' limited resources, modest education, and plebian tastes, they were determined to provide their children a loving home and an education. Every morning throughout our primary years, in rain, snow, sleet, or hail, Mother drove us to Saint Aloysius Gonzaga School in Cheektowaga, where we received a proper Catholic education from the nuns of Mount Saint Joseph Academy. We attended excellent Catholic high schools. I attended Canisius, the rigorous Jesuit school whose curriculum included four years of Latin and two years of a modern language. Mary Lee attended Mount Saint Joseph Academy, and Anne went to Holy Angels Academy, all schools with high academic standards. Although Father showed little interest in his children's studies, he worked hard at his many jobs to pay for the Catholic education that his children received, and I am sure that our parents sacrificed much to keep us in these schools. Yet this journey back to where I started would be incomplete if I did not confront my mother's statement and try to understand why it was at least partly true.

Take the Lionel train. Santa Claus delivered the initial set when I was four, and within only a few years, my father and I bonded closely through the annual ritual of setting up the layout and adding to it every Christmas. Whatever else passed between us during the rest of the year, however I disappointed him in other ways, or regardless of how preoccupied he was at other times in other seasons when I sought his attention, beginning in mid-November I knew that we would spend the next several weeks working on that model train nearly every night until the new layout was complete. We did not ask Mary Lee or Anne if they wanted to work on the layout, although I am sure that if asked, neither would have accepted. They saw the train as mine and as something that only boys and their fathers played with. That was the view of the Lionel Corporation, which featured in its catalogs photographs of wide-eyed boys and their pipe-smoking fathers looking over the latest rolling stock. No girls—or mothers—anywhere. Because I valued my father's attention and was enthralled by my ever-expanding layout, I did not question this male-only arrangement or reflect on its essential selfishness.

However, during the 1940s and 1950s, a significantly different paradigm was not possible. Sketching backwards from 2014, perhaps I should not chastise myself for acknowledging that I received more time and attention from Father than my sisters could have hoped for. Father and I built the train layout, attended Buffalo Bison baseball games, played catch in the yard, spent Saturday afternoons at Uncle

Frank's gas station, and worked together on repair projects that were not a "one-man job." This scenario is incomplete, because Father occasionally invited Mary Lee into his world. Like all superb carpenters, he had in his basement workshop a raft of tools and a wooden filing cabinet full of slim drawers that contained hundreds of nuts, bolts, screws, and assorted paraphernalia that he used on construction and repair projects. Mary Lee's task was to sort and organize these drawers so that he could always find exactly the nut or bolt or screw that he needed, and in this way, she helped him on his many projects, including building my attic bedroom. From her years spending time with him in his workshop, Mary Lee inherited knowledge of tools and a knack for repair work that few women of her generation have.

Mother spent many hours with Mary Lee and Anne, taking them to visit friends, to birthday parties, to the zoo and the beach, and to events at their elementary and high schools, and she invited their friends to our house to sleep over at slumber parties. They too received bicycles and roller and ice skates and books and new winter coats and hats and fuzzy socks. After Anne was born in 1950, Father built, at Mother's insistence, a playhouse in the backyard that we called "Little 490." It featured two windows and a Dutch door. Like the bedroom that Father built in the attic designed to fit my needs, so this miniature playhouse was especially tailored for his daughters. Mary Lee and Anne played with school and neighborhood friends and, in the summer, served them sandwiches and lemonade. In winter, Little 490 became a fort during our prodigious snowball fights, and it was a warming hut when we skated on the small ice rink that Father built every winter. During the coldest months of the year, Little 490 brought us kids and our parents together. I also remember Mary Lee and Anne receiving gifts like dolls and dollhouses and similar "girls' toys" for Christmas and birthdays. These perpetuated the gender roles that our parents envisioned for them and that never explicitly linked Father to their young lives.

I am sure that Mother sensed the disparities among her children's developing lives on Highgate, and I am equally sure that Father did not. Here I reach an impasse: I have no idea why my father was so blind to how differently he was treating his own children. Nor do I know now, at age seventy, why I was not more sensitive to what was happening deep within the collective psyche of this outwardly happy family. We had enjoyable times together—the Christmas holidays, family outings in all seasons, the trek to Muskoka, picnics and birthday parties and Halloween trick-or-treating, those interminable parades, and large family gatherings with Father's siblings at Grandma Shurgot's house or with Frank and

Henrietta Brown and assorted Irish relatives on Woodlawn Avenue. However, as Mary Lee and Anne grew, the distances between them and their father also grew.

Several years ago, Mary Lee told me of an incident from her childhood that magnifies the mystery of Father's parenting. Mother washed us and insisted that we change into clean clothes before Father came home from work. One summer day, when Anne was a baby, Mary Lee and I, all gussied up, met him in front of the house. Father picked me up and probably kissed me on the cheek. As Mary Lee remembers, as she held out her arms, rather than picking her up, Father stared at her as if he did not recognize her. No hug, no kiss. Assuming I was seven or eight, and Mary Lee five or six, the effect of this one bizarre moment must have been severe. What Mary Lee must have thought as a young child I cannot imagine and do not want to. Why no hug, no kiss? What separated her from me in our father's eyes? While this one incident was not the whole of Mary Lee's relationship with her father, it haunts her now in her late sixties. If asked then why he did not pick up his daughter, I doubt Father could have explained. As Mary Lee said to me, "I guess I spent most of my childhood always trying to please but never quite getting there." I have no answer now to the question of why this was so.

Mother encouraged Father to spend more time with Mary Lee and Anne. During that same visit to El Paso in 1976, Mother described an attempt to encourage Father to help Mary Lee learn to play golf. I played sandlot baseball, touch football, and ice hockey on our street, but Mary Lee never played sports at all, mostly because none of her friends did. Father was an excellent golfer who won several amateur tournaments in Buffalo, and for some reason, Mother decided that he could interest Mary Lee in golf and that she and he could then play together. (I had zero interest in golf, and Father knew it.)

One Sunday afternoon after church, when Mary Lee was probably ten or eleven, Mother begged Father to try to interest her in golf.

"Bill, look, I have a suggestion. Why don't you take Mary Lee into the backyard and maybe show her how to hit golf balls? She doesn't play any sports like Michael does, and maybe you and she could play together."

"Mary, I don't think she has any interest in golf. Why would I do that?"

"Well, it might be something you and she could share. You never know—she might be good at it. Why don't you just try? Just a few minutes. Would you do that for me?"

"Well, all right. I'll see what I can do."

Fifteen minutes later, Father was back inside reading his paper, complaining, as Mother explained, that Mary Lee "swung too hard." Mother said that her heart sank at Father's words. I imagined Mary Lee taking one entirely untutored, completely awkward swing with one of Father's clubs, and him walking away rather than commit to tutoring his own daughter in a game he knew well that they could have shared, however imperfectly, for many years. How ironic that he wanted to be a PE teacher! He spent hours with me refashioning the train layout one December after another for well into my high school years, but he could not spend fifteen minutes teaching his daughter how to swing a golf club. As a child, I had no grasp of the enormous distance that yawned between him and his older daughter. As I write these words, the realization of some of the ways that my father failed my sisters, Mary Lee especially, is painful. However, not knowing why he so consistently failed them is far more painful.

Even family events designed to bring us together ironically caused friction and resentment. In 1955, Father, Mary Lee, and I traveled on a special excursion train to Cleveland to see the Indians, with their talented center fielder Larry Doby, the first black player in the American League, play a doubleheader against the New York Yankees. I was twelve, and Mary Lee was ten.

We boarded the special excursion train at the ornate station on Pederewski Street in South Buffalo, and Mary Lee and I were thrilled by this journey to see a major league baseball game. The coach seats were two abreast; Father and I sat together, and Mary Lee sat alone. At the game, Father bought a scorecard so that we could follow all the at-bats of the Cleveland and New York players. I knew how to "score" a game, because Father showed me how the first time he took me to see the Buffalo Bison play at Offerman Stadium. Early in the game, maybe the second or third inning, I offered the scorecard to Mary Lee and asked her if she wanted to keep score, even though she had never been to a baseball game and did not know how. When she asked Father how to mark the scorecard, instead of explaining the process, he took the scorecard away from her and gave it to me. Again, Mary Lee was slighted for reasons she did not understand. Girls were not supposed to be baseball fans? Were not supposed to know how to mark a scorecard? Mother probably convinced Father to take Mary Lee on this trip, and I suspect that he resented having to take his daughter along on this "father-son" excursion to see a ball game.

Other incidents evinced a similar pattern. Mother arranged for Mary Lee and me to take piano lessons. When the television arrived in 1953, Father set it against the west wall of the living room. The piano was along the same wall of the former sitting room, a few feet from the corner of the TV. Friction between our practice time and TV viewing arose; Mary Lee and I wanted to practice after dinner, and Father wanted to plop into his chair by the fireplace and read his paper or watch TV. As Mary Lee was usually the one ordered to stop practicing, she ceased her lessons. (I quit because I wanted to play baseball—more on that fantasy later.) Mother observed all of this but said nothing.

In spring of 1962, my freshman year at Canisius College, I came home one day to learn that Mary Lee was pregnant. The father was Charles Joseph Brand ("Butch"), a young Italian fellow that she had been seeing for several months. When I arrived home that afternoon, Mary Lee was crying, Mother was hysterical, and Anne was dazed. My childhood careened through my mind. What I had sensed but darkly in the mirror of our family—Father's persistent slighting and at times neglect of Mary Lee, and the privileges I received—blazed brightly. I called Father at work and said to him, "This is our entire fault." He said "yes" and abruptly hung up. I realized instantly that Mary Lee—the rebellious, difficult second child, a daughter who swung a golf club too hard—had sought in the arms of another man the attention that she craved but did not receive from her father. A classic Freudian pattern—the daughter's search for the missing father—became real. Dinner that evening was funereal. Mary Lee did not look into her parents' eyes, they never looked up from their plates, and Anne and I were terrified to speak. After dinner, Mother cried, Father sulked, Anne and I escaped to our rooms, and no one said goodnight. Lying in bed, I heard my parents screaming at each other as I had never heard before and never heard again.

My reaction to this sudden intrusion into our family, into my childhood illusion of an ordered family life, was to escape. That spring, I went to a priest at Canisius and inquired about joining the Jesuits. For years, Mother's Aunt Nana had asked when I was going to begin studying for the priesthood. Nana believed that every Irish family ought to produce one priest for the propagation of the faith. I was the only boy in the extended family and, in her eyes, destined to become Father Michael. Mary Lee's pregnancy propelled me toward this vocation, this calling that became a retreat from my exaggerated sense of the chaos that had descended upon us. Somewhere along the line of laborious interviews imposed by the Jesuit Order, I stumbled and was told that I did not have a vocation. True; I didn't. Rather than helping with this growing challenge to our family, I was trying to flee, but from what? From my own selfishness? From Father's neglect of Mary Lee? From the enormous pain that plagued Mother? All of this surely.

One night, I went into the attic and hurled several Lionel freight cars against the wall, convinced that these toys symbolized a retreat into which Father and I had escaped for too many years and a familial innocence forever lost.

Well, not quite. I exaggerate. Mary Lee and Butch were married in a lovely ceremony at Saint Aloysius Church in July 1962. Mother and Father initially resented Butch and saw him, as did I, as an intruder into the family. Father did escort Mary Lee, arm in arm, down the aisle of our church to meet her husband. Once Mary Lee and Butch were married, Mother and Father swallowed their pride and their Roman Catholic righteousness, because they knew that Mary Lee desperately needed their love and support. By then Aunt Kay and Mother's Aunt Nana were gone, and Mary Lee and Butch had little money and few resources, so Mother decided that they could move into the downstairs bedroom that Mary Lee and I had shared as children. (I can imagine that conversation: Father screaming "Hell no!" and Mother calmly asking the obvious question, "Well now Bill, where else can they go?")

Notwithstanding another assault on Father's fervent desire to spend his evenings sitting quietly by the fireplace, the house on Highgate opened its creaky doors to another growing family, and again its rhythms changed, though not without difficulty. Once Mary Lee's daughter, Christine, was born that October, there were two interrelated yet distinct families sharing four bedrooms and one small bathroom. Every evening, there were two dinners: one for Mother, Father, Anne, and myself and one later for Mary Lee, Butch, and Christine. Because Butch was Italian, Mary Lee prepared many spicy Italian meals that permeated the entire house. Father scoffed one night that the house—*his* house!—smelled like an Italian café. There were never enough clean plates or silverware. Baby bottles were left to dry every night on the kitchen table where Father ate breakfast. If Butch—who worked construction when he worked at all—had to be on a job at six o'clock in the morning, he and Father competed for bathroom space. He had less competition for the bathroom when Mother insisted that he share it with ducks!

Besides the cramped conditions, other tensions percolated among the three generations now living together. All of us accepted that a breach had opened within our family. Indeed, for the two years that Mary Lee and her family lived among us, we all learned, slowly and painfully, a new definition of that word "family." Many nights when Father came home from work, especially before Christine was born, he did not acknowledge Butch's presence, and Butch and Mary Lee retreated to their back bedroom in an eerie silence. Father sulked, and Mother chatted aimlessly trying to cheer him, which inevitably increased the friction between them. Many nights during dinner, I nervously waited for Father to explode at what he considered Mary Lee's betrayal and Butch's invasion. Butch was Father's son-in-law, though not one he would have chosen, and he did help with chores around the house. Butch was much taller and much stronger than I was so he was especially good at helping Father install storm windows. Butch shoveled the sidewalks in winter and mowed the lawn in summer, and he talked with Father and me about sports, especially baseball. On weekends, Mary Lee often cooked huge dinners for all of us, and I remember wonderful Italian meals at Butch's parents' house, featuring Mrs. Brand's delicious meatballs and many bottles of red wine. In these little ways, we all tried to grow closer together and to see beyond the embarrassment, anger, and pain of those first few crowded months on Highgate.

Mary Lee, Butch, and Christine lived with us until the fall of 1964 when they got their own apartment. Mother and Father gradually realized that they had a second chance to show love for their daughter by loving her own family. They, Anne, and I learned to know—and to love—Mary Lee all over again, now as a wife and mother as well as a daughter and sister. As I realized Christine's profound importance to Mary Lee, I, who had tried to abandon this family that I had cherished so deeply, developed a far greater understanding of love. Many years earlier, Mary Lee had a white mouse that she kept in a cardboard box. Among the Highgate menagerie, this mouse was exclusively hers. When one of our damn cats caught and ate that tiny mouse, Mary Lee was devastated. During a conversation in the back yard, late in her pregnancy, Mary Lee told me that having a child in her womb was like having that mouse so many years before: the child was exclusively hers. I believe that Christine became Mary Lee's salvation, a possession that no one could take from her.

When my parents and Anne moved to Canton, Ohio, in the summer of 1966, Mary Lee, Butch, along with Christine, their son Jay, and their second daughter Lisa moved back to Highgate and renewed the cycle of family life. The physical distance between Mary Lee and our parents ironically became restorative, and family visits with grandchildren gradually healed the psychological distance that had developed over the years. During Mary Lee's marriage, Father became more responsive and affectionately called her "Kiddo." He accepted his grandchildren as part of his extended family, and when Mary Lee's marriage crumbled in the mid-1970s, Father comforted her in ways that neither would have thought possible a few years before. Father's last words to Mary Lee before he died were "You'll be okay, Kiddo." Indeed she was; and is.

Father once said of Mary Lee that she should have had a revolution to lead. Had she started somewhere else, she might have had such an opportunity, but not in our house on Highgate. Instead of a revolution, she started a family of which she and her parents became justly proud. Mary Lee and Butch were married for fourteen years, during which she and, for several years Butch, succeeded in creating a loving family on Highgate. Her children are well educated, prosperous, and happy. In the essential task of her life, Mary Lee succeeded brilliantly.

In 1969 my wife Gail and I spent the Christmas holiday with my parents in Canton. Anne was enrolled at Kent State University, where two years later four students would be shot dead by Guardsmen during antiwar rallies. A few days before Christmas, while talking to Mother in my parents' bedroom, I noticed a guitar under the bed. Puzzled, I asked her whom the guitar was for. She said it was for Anne. I said that I did not know that Anne had an interest in music or in playing a guitar. She said, "Well, we thought maybe she would like a guitar, and we are trying to make up for not having given Mary Lee as many gifts as we should have." I was shocked! Not only was Mother admitting, rather crudely, a neglect of her first daughter but also *quantifying* love toward a child in ways I never expected her to admit. Mother and Father probably believed that giving Anne gifts of a kind that Mary Lee never received would show their love for Anne, and for that I cannot fault them. The combination of admitting their perceived neglect of Mary Lee, plus their belief that material gifts to one child as an indication of love could somehow ameliorate their lack of giving to another, was heartbreaking. As had happened the second I knew that Mary Lee was pregnant, my relationships with my siblings on Highgate blazed before me. I stood there, married, in my mid-Twenties, hoping to have my own family, and hearing Mother admit that the parents I deeply loved recognized that they had been insufficiently attentive to their second child and were now trying to compensate materially for that neglect. I still experience that awful moment viscerally and wonder why it happened.

My sisters and I never doubted that our parents loved each other. Nor do I believe, despite all of the above, that we doubted that they loved their children.

Parenting in any generation is terribly difficult. Looking back on these few incidents and on my parents as the complex human beings they were—their European heritage, their traditional notions of parental responsibility, their often-constrained economic circumstances, their different expectations for male and female children, their immersion in American mores of the late 1940s and 1950s, Mother's enthusiasm, humor, and warmth clashing with Father's reticence, practicality, and shyness—I realize that perhaps I am being overly critical of them and too severe with myself. Case in point. In June 1965, my senior year in college, I actually had a date for the senior prom, itself an accomplishment, and I needed the car to pick her up. About 6:30 p.m., I came out of the bathroom and stood next to the kitchen door. I told my date I would pick her up at 7:00 p.m., and as I would soon be ready to leave, I asked Mother, who was sitting at the kitchen table, if the car was ready. She said no, because Mary Lee had gone to get some groceries for my graduation party that weekend. I was angry because Mary Lee wasn't back yet, and I blurted, "This is the most important night of my college career. I can't be late!" or some such nonsense! Mother started to cry, and suddenly, but again too late, I realized why. Mary Lee, who had never finished high school and already had two children, was out getting stuff for my graduation party, and all I could do was complain because she hadn't yet returned. How monstrously selfish that moment now appears to me!

Perhaps these specific incidents, and the history they encapsulate, were less damaging, or less revelatory, than I imagine them to have been. Children must deal with both their environment and their genetic inheritance, but they also make choices that affect their adult lives. They heed or refuse advice that is intended for their own good, often regardless of how that advice is tendered. They do or do not seize opportunities for education and/or employment. They choose their own companions and interact among them as they wish. One can never completely understand why one's siblings chose their paths, just as one cannot competently assert that one's siblings would have been better off had they chosen different paths. What right do I have to make such a claim? No one can start from somewhere else, and certainly during my sisters' adult and our parents' later lives they exchanged much love. Anne once told me that during her years in Canton, she could have used more guidance from Mother and Father, but as the only child then living with her parents they gradually grew closer together than they had been on Highgate. As they had in Buffalo, they paid for Anne to attend an excellent high school, Eastside Catholic. After the shootings at Kent State University, Mother and Father rushed to the campus to bring Anne home, and though she never returned to university, she found love and comfort in her parents' home and the courage to go on with her life despite that horrible episode. When Mary Lee's marriage disintegrated, Father filled the emotional void in her life and became a caring grandfather to her children. When Mother lapsed into her final illness, destitute and without health insurance, Mary Lee (and Anne, during visits from Ohio) nursed her lovingly. From the gaze into the kaleidoscope of our lives, where history and memory whirl incessantly, I realize how much I loved our parents for what they tried, however imperfectly, to do for their children. No child should expect more.

Did Father love his children? Yes. Did he know how to show that love? Not really. Did he damage his children? To some degree, and variously, yes. Was that his fault? We are who we are. Have I judged him too harshly? Perhaps. We all bestow love in our own ways. We might wish that one or both of our parents cherished us more openly, more consistently, more selflessly, or more tenderly. Looking back now as a parent myself, I can recognize my father struggling to show affection, and his intense desire for privacy and solitude must have made this effort immensely difficult.

The night in April 1975 that Mother called me in Madison to tell me Father's cancer was so advanced that, after exploratory surgery, the doctors had sewed him back together to let him die, I had a terrifying nightmare: my son, Nicholas, then two, was dying. Instead of being the son losing his father, I was the father losing his son, and he was unable to tell me that he loved me. Why this nightmare? Perhaps my subconscious projected into my present life my fear that my dying father did not know that I loved him. From the late 1960s into the early 1970s, we had quarreled about the civil rights movement, the war in Vietnam, and especially my decision—*after* getting married and spending eight months flat broke as a VISTA volunteer in Oregon—to pursue a PhD rather than go to work and act "responsibly." The last time I saw him, the morning in August 1975 that Gail and I and our kids left Canton for El Paso, I said, "Dad, I love you." And I do.

CHAPTER 4:
ODYSSEUS IN THE SNOW

—ɷ—

From spring 1953 through summer 1960, I had a morning paper route delivering the *Buffalo Courier-Express*. The paper was published 365 days a year, and during those seven years I rose daily about 5:00 a.m. to complete my route on Highgate between Bailey Avenue and Eggert Road. I had about sixty customers, and they expected their paper before 7:00 a.m. regardless of the weather conditions. I could not sleep in lest my daily schedule, especially during the school year, collapsed before it began. Unless I was really sick, we were heading to Muskoka, or I had cajoled one of the Dressel kids into taking the route for a few days, every morning Brandy and I traveled up and down Highgate, delivering to my slumbering customers the news of Buffalo and the world.

The papers arrived in a large, green box in front of the house. Brandy had superb hearing, and every morning when he heard the delivery man open and then slam shut the lid, he stirred and woke me to begin our journey. For most of the year, I carried the papers slung in a sack over my shoulder as I rode my clunky Schwinn bicycle from house to house, tossing papers on front porches or sliding them behind screen doors. As Odysseus sailed among the Greek isles on his perilous journey, I skillfully maneuvered through, under, or around daunting obstacles: narrow driveways, parked cars, low-hanging tree limbs, baby strollers, sporting goods, and kids' toys strewn haphazardly across front steps. Accompanied by my faithful companion who knew the way, I ventured forth from home, persevered through rain, sleet, hail, heat, and, from early December through late March, snow upon snow. Most of the year—spring, summer, and fall—I completed my mission and returned home in about forty-five minutes.

Winter, however, demanded greater fortitude. Snowfalls of six to eight inches were not uncommon, nor were single-digit temperatures. On very cold mornings, when Brandy stirred I hesitated because I knew what awaited me. We usually awoke around 5:00, but when a heavy snowfall was expected the night before I set the alarm for as early as 4:30. Because Father always turned the furnace down before going to bed, on many winter mornings I awoke in a room so cold that frost covered the *inside* of the double-pane windows. Sliding from under two life-preserving Hudson Bay blankets into this frigid air required precise timing and carefully sequenced movements. As Brandy yawned and stretched at the foot of the bed, I gazed at my dresser, remembering in which drawer I kept my wool sweaters, socks, and long johns, then glanced at the closet where my coat, hat, and snow pants hung. I had to be sure that the door was open.

I bolted from bed, tore off pajamas, darted stark naked to the dresser, opened the drawer, pulled on wool socks, top and bottom long johns, two shirts, two sweaters, and flannel-lined jeans, then ran to the closet for snow pants, a wool cap and winter coat, its pockets bulging with two pairs of gloves. Armored against the elements, Brandy and I dashed through the even colder attic and downstairs into the kitchen where I gulped down a glass of—what else?—cold milk before donning my boots to head outside—or try to. A heavy snowfall meant that before I got to the paper box I struggled with the side door that was jammed shut. Many a winter morning, Brandy, unable to wait until I opened the damn door, peed in the hall. Once to the box, I quickly loaded the papers into my sack and trudged off, muffled against the stinging cold and guided by my coal-black dog that stood out boldly against the snow. These winter treks were heroic: Brandy bounding ahead of me, forging a path, I bravely bearing my load and high stepping in the deep, relentless snow. We were solitary travelers in a great white wilderness, roaming among the wind-whipped mounds of snow that crunched beneath my boots, step after step from house to house, summoning winter's most distinct sound. By five-thirty or six on winter mornings, the only signs of life in the neighborhood were the tracks that marked our lonely journey through the sleeping world.

Obstacles abounded. If a plow had come through the day before, huge piles of snow buried the sidewalks on both sides of Highgate for the length of my route. Scaling these piles, block after block, demanded strength and courage. No sane person shovels before 5:00 a.m., so a heavy snowfall overnight often obliterated the outlines of porch steps while concealing a layer of treacherous ice below. I often slipped on this hidden ice and cascaded akimbo down the steps. On Sundays, when the papers were much heavier and I couldn't carry them in my sack, I loaded them precariously on a sled, terrified that as I hauled it over the ragged mounds of snow the sled would tip and scatter the intricately folded papers that I knew I could never reassemble. Even with help from one of the Dressel kids, the Sunday route in winter seemed endless. Despite the innumerable layers of clothing, by the time I reached home most of my body was cold.

If I complained about the elements, Mother assured me that crawling out of bed at 4:30 to deliver the paper would make me a stronger and better person. When I asked her, "How?" she rambled about character building, taking responsibility, and overcoming hardship. I developed healthy lungs, strong legs, and a respect for winter, all of which proved immensely beneficial when I started climbing Washington State's glaciated mountains in my mid-fifties. I also learned that one should finish what one has started, whether it was a graduate degree, a book manuscript, a twelve-thousand-foot climb, or a marriage. I sometimes wonder, however, how many of life's important lessons I might have learned playing chess.

As I reflect now on that experience, I realize that having a morning paper route in Buffalo was primarily a spiritual experience. Being Irish Catholic, my mother convinced her children that life would be hard because God—as in yester years Zeus—sent us trials that, like Odysseus, we had to endure. If we succeeded in these trials, especially the wintry ones—if we stayed the course between the snow of Scylla and the cold of Charybdis—did not lose faith or quit, we would be rewarded, if not in this life then surely in the next, which I began to suspect was in Florida. The longer I delivered the *Courier-Express* on those formidable winter mornings, the more I believed that heavy snowfalls and frigid temperatures, along with Brandy's faulty bladder, were gifts that God sent to me because He genuinely cared for my spiritual welfare. Like Homer's wandering hero, at the end of each winter route—tired, wet, and cold—I reveled in my successful return home.

Mother's exhortations on the virtues of having a morning paper route also led me to petition God about the spiritual state of my best friends on the street, Danny Miller and the Dressel brothers. Every night, I knelt next to my bed and earnestly pleaded with God to arrange for Danny and the Dressels to get a morning paper route. Figuring that I already had a leg up on salvation, I wasn't about to relinquish mine, but I thought that an opening might develop somewhere else in the neighborhood, maybe on Winspear or Rounds or Lisbon, and God could arrange for my buddies to get a route. Getting a morning route, even if they had to share it, would signal that they too were potentially blessed by its rigors and hardships. A few years after I began my petition drive, Danny Miller got a *Buffalo Evening News* route on Highgate, delivering the paper six days per week between 4:00 and 5:00 p.m., a time by which, even after one of Buffalo's legendary snowfalls, most people would have shoveled their driveways and sidewalks even if plows had been through earlier in the day. The Dressel brothers never did get a route.

Despite my faith in the righteousness of God's will and the piety of my prayers, I remained bewildered by the unanswered existential question of who is chosen to get what paper route in cold, snowy Buffalo, and how being chosen or not might be related to one's spiritual destiny. I learned to accept my lot, to persevere through whatever winter threw at me, to be grateful for the chance to prove my worthiness, and to pray for an early spring.

CHAPTER 5:
A BOX OF MEDALS

—◊—

SENIOR EIGHT, WESTSIDE ROWING CLUB, 1930;
BILL SHURGOT COXSWAIN

My bedroom was not as wide as the attic itself. On both sides, between the exterior walls and the slope of the roof, were corridors as long as the bedroom and about two feet wide. The only light in the attic was a single 100-watt bulb with no shade that hung on a long chain from the ceiling. This provided enough light to see when going from the attic door to my room, but its light did not shine into the side corridors that were always dark and contributed to my sense of the attic being, like the basement, a scary place. Who knew what was hidden in these narrow places? Maybe some of the Little People (who I believed frequented the basement and raided my mother's vegetable jars and canned fruit every winter) also lived in the deep, dark corridors right next to my bedroom. Heading to bed on winter nights, when I sensed that some of these visitors might be about the house, I slowly opened the attic door, reached around to the left to flip the light switch, and dashed to my bedroom door before anyone could grab me.

One spring afternoon in 1953, when I had become intensely curious about all the stuff my parents stored in these corridors, I decided to investigate.

Stooping to fit into the narrow spaces, armed with a flashlight and wary of what I might find, I poked around in the cardboard boxes, suitcases, and cedar chests stacked along the walls. Most of what I found was predictable: faded photographs of relatives, discarded clothes that my parents couldn't relinquish, partially broken toys no longer wanted, old books, Halloween costumes, perhaps being saved for grandchildren, old tools and cutlery sets. Nothing remarkable. In an old cedar chest that contained memorabilia, photos, and yearbooks from my father's years at Bennett High School in Buffalo and Normal College of Indiana, I found a small, elaborately carved cedar box with brass hinges and a brass latch. It was unlocked. I was immediately curious, as it was beautifully carved and well preserved, suggesting an exotic case of valuable treasures. Holding the box under my arm and careful not to spill its contents, I slowly made my way out of the corridor and back into the attic proper.

The contents of the box deeply influenced my adolescence. Inside were red and blue ribbons attached to gleaming gold, silver, and bronze medals etched with words that evoked a world of athletic triumphs:

> *First Place: Boys 400 Meter Relay-Buffalo High School Swimming Championships 1927*
> *AAU Champion: Platform Diving 1931*
> *AAU Champion: Free Style 100 Meters 1930*
> *First Place: AAU Fencing-120 LB Division 1919*
> *Second Place: Men's Senior Eight-Canadian Henley Regatta 1930*
> *First Place: Men's Senior Four with Coxswain;West Side Rowing Club Regatta 1930*

Carefully preserved in this beautifully crafted box were medals from my father's prodigious accomplishments in swimming, diving, fencing, and rowing from high school through college. Hidden in this dark corridor of the attic, like a secret treasure, this precious casket of gold, silver, and bronze illuminated an earlier part of my father's life. Holding these medals in my hands, I imagined him as he was then: athletic, strong, and confident, not the reserved, reclusive man who often seemed overwhelmed by Mother's relentless energy and the responsibilities of parenting. Here was an image of Father that I vowed to emulate and that I believed would make him proud of me. I would become an athlete: swim, dive, and play second base like the fabled Jackie Robinson, or coxy an eight-oared shell to victory at the Canadian Henley Regatta or at Buffalo's West

Side Rowing Club, where later I would find his name on plaques honoring his victorious crews.

My dreams of athletic prowess took many forms, many of them predictable for an urban kid in the 1950s. The first was baseball. The American poet Donald Hall defines baseball as "fathers and sons playing catch," and Father and I had started playing catch when I was young, perhaps seven or eight. We played first with a tennis ball in the narrow alley between our house and old man Hennsler's, and it was there that my dreams of heroism began. Having received from my father the gene for loving underdogs, I was born a Brooklyn Dodgers fan, and when we played catch, I wore a Dodgers cap. On fly balls hit to center field, dangerously close to Hennsler's living room window, I became the Dodgers' center fielder, Duke Snider. On ground balls to the infield, I became my idol, Jackie Robinson, the Dodgers' electric second baseman who played the position for which I was practicing. There was magic in that Dodgers' cap. It was a talisman that, if I practiced religiously, would someday transport me to the hallowed ground of Ebbets Field.

My first organized form of baseball was a game that Danny Miller, the Dressel brothers and I played called "Strike Out." Kids all over America played this. All we needed was a baseball bat and a bunch of socks rolled tightly together and bound with layers of heavy twine and tape. We played in the back yard of whichever parents weren't hanging out the wash or gardening that day. As the backyards on Highgate were small and rectangular, we easily imagined them as a baseball park, complete with the small patch of grass as the outfield. At our house, the pitcher stood in the middle of the driveway in front of the garage, the batter stood where the driveway opened onto the wider parking slab, dangerously close to the window of the back bedroom, and the outfielder, the other part of the two-man team, stood in the yard near the back fence. The rules were equally simple and contentious. Home plate was a piece of cardboard, and the pitcher called balls and strikes, provoking constant arguments between pitcher and batter that delayed our games immeasurably.

"Strike three! Yer out."

"That was high and inside."

"No, it wasn't. You ducked. That ain't fair."

"I hadda duck, or it woulda hit me."

"You stand too close to the plate. Move back!"

A sock-ball caught on the fly by the outfielder was an out. Because there wasn't room for three bases, we used another piece of cardboard for first base, which in our yard was right in front of the garage. If the sock-ball was hit on the ground, the pitcher or fielder could get the batter out if he hit him racing to first with the sock before he reached the cardboard "base." The pitcher or fielder also called out or safe, provoking further arguments.

"I got you. Yer out!"

"I beat the throw. I'm safe."

"No, ya didn't.

"Did too. Look, here's the base. I touched the corner."

"The base moved. I got ya. Yer out!"

"Ah shit!"

This game seems innocent enough, but one day it nearly killed me. George Dressel, the strongest kid on the block, and I were on the same team. His brother, Paul, threw a pitch high and inside, and I was sure that George would not swing at it, so I stood up to catch it. George swung, missed the sock, smacked me just above my left eye, and knocked me out cold. Mary Lee, who chronicled my athletic foibles, raced into the house and announced to Mother, "Well, he's dead this time!" I woke up an hour later flat on the couch with a monstrous headache, a doctor bending over me, blind in my left eye, and sporting a hideous bulge of black and blue flesh. Mother told me weeks later that the doctor had told her that I was lucky. Had George's bat landed an inch lower, it would have demolished my left eye. Needless to say, I was benched for the rest of the season.

There were other forms of baseball. Once we all had bicycles, we organized a game that we considered "real" baseball. We invited kids from neighboring streets, assembled in front of my house, and with Brandy racing along and dodging cars, we rode—sans helmets!—down to the corner of Bailey and Main and set up a baseball diamond on the green fields of the University of Buffalo. We lugged stakes and ropes to create the outfield wall, used heavy cardboard for the bases, and a slab of rubber that we found one day for the pitcher's mound. With maybe six or seven kids on a side, we played for hours. We always forgot to bring an umpire, so the arguments about balls and strikes and safe or out were interminable. We created a sense of an actual baseball field, with an outfield wall (well, rope), home plate, three bases, and a real baseball and bats. Although in all my years of playing I got maybe four hits—all singles—pedaling to that green field meant that at a crucial moment in that day's game, I might connect on a fastball in the bottom of the ninth and belt it deep over the left field rope. I would narrate to my father a heroic tale of the winning blast that would propel me one step closer to Ebbets Field.

On summer evenings, neighborhood kids gathered at the large playground up Highgate at PS 80 to play softball games that we called "Choose Up." The cinder playground was large enough to rival a real baseball field, with real rubber bases, a pitching mound, a home plate, and steel fences down both the left and right field lines. We gathered around 6:30 p.m., and two of the older boys began the ritual of choosing sides that began each game. One kid tossed a bat, handle up, to another who caught it as close as possible to the bottom. They alternately worked sets of fingers up toward the knob of the bat, the object being to create a space at the top where the other kid could not insert any fingers, not even one, between the top of the other's hand and the knob of the bat. Whoever got any number of fingers right under the knob of the bat first had first choice of players, hence the moniker "Choose Up." After the first choice, always the best hitter, the two "captains" alternately chose other players until everyone was on one of the teams: "Joe. Sam. Tom. Bill. Bobby. Tony. Dick. Sean. Rick. Paul." If there were more than eighteen kids, the extras were subs that might or might not get into the game. This was serious competition!

I stood on the perimeter of this ritual and was chosen, if at all, last. Skinny, short, and wearing thick glasses, I hardly looked athletic. I had a ratty old glove from somewhere, maybe from my cousin Craig, and lacking even rudimentary hand-eye coordination, I couldn't hit worth a damn. I swung hard but with my eyes deep in left field, where I imagined my home runs sailing away, rather on the ball I was trying to hit. I never connected. If chosen, I wanted to play second base but was exiled to right field, the designated position for kids who could not catch. There were some left-handed hitters in Buffalo, but as they seldom came to PS 80, I seldom fielded a hit. I was benched when a superior player showed up, and I never played a whole game. Trudging home every night, head down, Dodgers cap in one hand, tattered glove in the other, having struck out my one time at bat and being benched for most of the game, I mustered the courage to return the next night, believing—somehow—that I would play better.

In 1955, the year of the Dodgers' stupendous World Series victory over the Yankees, I got my big break. Father gave me a new baseball glove for my birthday, and I was determined to make an actual team. I hoped to make a team in the Babe Ruth League, and on the last day of tryouts, while playing second base, I made a diving stop of a hot grounder to my right, stood, and threw out the runner. After practice, I was told that based on this one dazzling play, I had made the team, albeit as a second-string (if not third-string) infielder. That night I was ebullient at the dinner table. Over and over I described my sterling play, and I proudly showed Father my uniform. I was on a real team that practiced on a real baseball diamond! I was an athlete!

Halfway through the season, after warming the bench for six games, I went in to play second base in the fifth inning of a game my team was losing badly. I played one inning, fielded one ground ball, and threw out the runner. Yes! Shades of Jackie! In the next inning, I came up to bat. I swung and missed at the first two pitches. Needing to relax and refocus, I stepped out of the batter's box, took a deep breath, and stepped back in. As the next pitch whizzed past me, the ump yelled, "Strike three!" Three pitches—the last one a called strike—and I was out. I was so frustrated at my failure that I shouted "Oh bullshit!" at the ump, who promptly threw me out of the game. I was done for the season. I never played another game of organized baseball. I became content with our ragtag games on the green fields at Bailey and Main or the occasional stint in right field on the cinders at PS 80.

There were other games such as "Whiffle Ball Strike Out," where every kid threw a nasty knuckleball, and touch football played until dusk in the middle of Highgate until the cops showed up and threatened to take away our equipment because some cranky neighbor had complained about the noise. Every winter, after the first snow had frozen and the streets became sheets of ice, we set up goals made of two-by-fours nailed together and played hockey with homemade sticks. Because the sticks were made of thin slabs of wood screwed or nailed into one-by-twos, and we played with a real puck, the sticks never lasted long, and I spent more time in the basement with my father's tools trying to fix broken sticks than actually playing hockey. Miraculously, none of us suffered permanent damage to our gonads when playing goalie. We were wonderfully inventive for all four seasons, and while I never excelled at our games, in my imagination every game in every season—even snowball fights!—presented another chance for athletic excellence.

Entering Canisius High School in 1957 gave me more opportunities to compete in organized sports. I tried out for the swimming and diving teams in my freshman year, mainly because I knew that my father had excelled at these sports. I had never been a strong swimmer, and I lacked sufficient coordination and body control to dive gracefully. I dreaded the bus ride home the afternoon I was cut from both teams. I knew that when I got home, Father would ask me about practice, and I would have to admit the truth. When I told him, he said, "Well, that's okay, at least you tried," and while he was being kind, I was humiliated. I had failed at the sports at which I knew he had excelled, and in his silence that evening, I felt his disappointment.

CANISIUS HIGH SCHOOL JUNIOR-VARSITY EIGHT, 1960; AUTHOR KNEELING

I did make the Canisius rowing team as a coxswain in the spring of 1958, mainly because I was short and light and—like my mother—loud. I stayed with rowing for three enjoyable years, coxying first freshmen, then junior varsity, and eventually varsity shells in regattas at Buffalo's West Side Rowing Club, on the Detroit River, and at Saint Catherine's, Ontario, site of the annual Canadian Henley Schoolboy Regatta. In the spring of 1960 I was part of the most exciting and rewarding athletic experience of my life. The coach, Charley Fontana, recognized championship potential in the school's Senior Four with Cox. That spring, Charley worked relentlessly the four rowers—Paul Salm, Bill Schmidt, Kevin White, and Mike Peck—because he knew that to win a national title, a crew had to maximize its strength and synchronize its rhythms until the four oarsmen blended into a single indomitable force. As one of the crew's two coxswains, my main physical challenge was to lose weight, so I ran with the rowers every day and followed a restrictive diet. Many nights, dinner was a large bowl of cottage cheese and two glasses of orange juice. Charley had us on the water even before all the ice was gone from the Black Rock Channel, and as the American and Canadian championships approached, he had us rowing six or seven days a week. We even rowed at 8:00 a.m. on Easter Sunday! While Mother was aghast at my spending Easter morning pounding out rhythms for the rowers, Father thought this commitment to crew was marvelous.

My practice, dedication, and ice dodging were greatly rewarded. Our Canisius High Senior Four won the US National Schoolboy Championship in Philadelphia, with John Fraunheim as coxswain, and with me at the helm and my parents in the grandstand, the Canadian Henley Schoolboy Championship in St. Catherine's. Father was waiting for me when I steered our shell back to the dock, and he cheered when the rowers hurled me, arms and legs flying, into the water, the traditional reward for winning coxswains. That crew thus claimed the title of the best high school four with coxswain in North America, and I was immensely proud to have been part of that team.

Having won a few junior varsity four and eight-oared victories, and having been a member of the international champion varsity four, I was awarded a varsity letter at the annual athletic awards celebration. Father and I attended the ceremony on a Tuesday night in the Canisius auditorium. Sitting next to him, waiting for coach to call my name to receive my letter, I was ecstatic. I was going to receive a varsity letter in crew, one of my father's premier sports, in front of all my classmates and in my father's presence! When Mr. Fontana called my name, I floated down the aisle to receive the certificate. I was *so* proud! Here at last was a physical symbol of athletic accomplishment! I treasured the large gold "C" with the blue border and the blue oars crossed through the center to signify crew, and I could not wait to have it sewn onto the white wool sweater that I ordered from Broadway Knitting Mills. The letter would be above the left pocket with "Mike" written above the right pocket in blue-and-gold script.

The sweater arrived two weeks later. I could not wait for Father to come home so I could show it to him. We agreed that it was beautiful, and that night, after modeling it for the whole family, I placed it back in the shipping box to keep it clean.

I wore the sweater for the first time, over a pressed white shirt and tie, the day that the photo of the crew team was taken for the yearbook. I couldn't wait to get to school! The yearbook photo would capture forever an image that I was sure Father would cherish: his son, co-coxswain of the famous Canisius High School Senior Four that had won both Canadian and American championships, in his white varsity letter sweater emblazoned with the gold "C" and the blue oars. After that memorable day, one of the proudest of my young life, I wore the sweater occasionally. However, to my chagrin, I gradually discovered that because I earned it as a coxswain, who basically sits on his ass steering and yelling while the big guys row furiously, I was not considered an "athlete" by most students. Track and field participants, basketball, baseball and football players, and rowers were athletes; they expended energy and endured pain and were considered worthy of their letter sweaters. One day several hefty football players openly laughed at me when they saw me wearing the sweater in the cafeteria. I was unbearably humiliated and couldn't wait to leave school. When I got home, I unceremoniously stuffed the sweater into the bottom drawer of my dresser and never wore it again. I knew that I was banishing forever the one visible symbol of my efforts to emulate my father's athleticism, but I could not tolerate others' ridicule of it.

Sometime later, for reasons I never understood, my mother washed the sweater. The blue of the oars and yellow of the "C" bled into the pocket. The sweater was ruined. It was perhaps a fitting end to an athletic career that was mostly, except for one grand moment in St. Catherine's, a blur of disappointments. I had garnered a few medals while on the rowing team but not nearly enough to fill even a small cedar box.

Although my parents saw my win at Henley, it was one of the few races that Father attended, and I have often wondered why he did not attend more. In my senior year and for two years at Canisius College, I ran cross-country. I was not especially fast, but I could maintain a steady pace for many miles, and I loved the rhythm of long-distance running. Despite my competiveness in this sport, Father never showed much interest in it; he came to one race.

All children try to please their parents in any way they can. As adults, we realize that the effort should be its own reward, but in the imagination of a young boy, eager to please his athletic father, that trove of gold, silver, and bronze medals was immensely powerful. My desperate efforts to impress my father undoubtedly originated in an attempt to solidify our relationship. I also wonder if those efforts were subconsciously designed to resurrect the assertive, confident man I imagined when I marveled at those shining medals and colorful ribbons. If so, my efforts failed. For the remainder of my life in Buffalo, my father remained a quiet, reserved man. The box of medals remained in the attic, and my letter sweater lay crumbled in the bottom drawer of my dresser. The road from the green fields of my youth to Ebbets Field proved impossibly long, and perhaps Mother's ill-fated washing of the sweater was meant to cleanse my dreams of stardom.

Discovering that enchanting box in its dark, mysterious setting created an image of my father that I have always treasured, and I now believe that its mere existence, along with my sweater, somewhere in the house, was enough.

CHAPTER 6:
LATIN, GREEK, AND THE SONS OF IMMIGRANTS

—◊◊◊—

The last names of my classmates for four years at Canisius High School included the following: Abella, Baetzhold, Biondella, Buchinski, Barczuk, Cavalieri, DeNisco, Denny, DiMartino, Gautieri, Ganey, Goetz, Hajduk, Jaworski, Kwiatkowski, Lacey, Lenegan, Manias, McCarthy, Renda, Riforgiate, Rybuczeski, Schaus, Schnitter, Shultz, Sorrentino, Spicciati, Sroka, Steinagle, Subkoviak, Tryjankowski, and Zeis.

As Michael Lacey, a fellow CHS graduate, observes, our classmates were the sons of Europeans who immigrated in large numbers to industrialized American cities in the late-nineteenth and early-twentieth centuries. Most of the names are Polish or Italian, many are Irish, some are German, and some (like mine) are Ukrainian or other Eastern European. From any of the CHS yearbooks during my sojourn there (1961–1965), one could open to the pages of the homerooms or the list of seniors and find an equally compelling list of distinctively ethnic names. There were Smiths and Joneses among my classmates who lived mostly in the suburbs north and east of Buffalo, but the majority of the CHS students came from Buffalo's many ethnic enclaves. Despite this European heterogeneity, there were no blacks and few, if any, Jews.

Throughout my years in Buffalo, the Catholic education system flourished. Every neighborhood boasted at least one Catholic elementary and often two Catholic high schools. The elementary schools were attached by name and affiliation to a parish so that the academic subjects were supplemented by regular attendance at Mass and religious instruction from nuns and priests. In elementary school, children were instructed in the rigors of Confession, which meant, at the tender age of seven, being convinced that they were guilty of at least one venial sin that they had to confess to a priest in the dark, vaguely disturbing confessionals carved into the walls of every Catholic church. Once this confession was "satisfactorily completed" (I never knew how that was to be determined), children could take their First Communion and, a few years later, experience Confirmation, the third of the Sacraments of Initiation after Baptism and Communion. Completing these three sacraments meant that one was formally accepted into the Roman Catholic Church. These parish schools funneled students into the Catholic high schools operated by the Diocese of Buffalo or to private Catholic schools: Sacred Heart, Holy Angels, or Nardin Academy for girls; Canisius or its arch rival, Saint Joseph Academy, for boys. Given the large number of Catholic families of all nationalities in Buffalo, especially Polish, Italian, and Irish, this interlocked and closely monitored educational system ensured that freshman in any of the area's Catholic high schools had received a sound education in the Catholic faith and were accustomed to rigorous studies and high expectations from their teachers and parents.

Canisius stands in a long, heralded tradition of not only Roman Catholic but also specifically Jesuit education rooted in the educational philosophy of Ignatius Loyola, the sixteenth-century founder of the Jesuits. While cognizant of the need to prepare students for careers in the contemporary world, this tradition emphasizes a classical education that includes several humanities subjects: theology, philosophy, history, literature, logic, grammar and rhetoric, and language. When a CHS student reached the end of his sophomore year, he had to choose from among three curricular tracks for his junior and senior years: general education, science emphasis, or Greek emphasis. The most remarkable feature of all three tracks was the language requirement. All students in the general education or science emphasis had to take two years of a modern European language (I chose German), while students choosing the Greek emphasis, whom everyone rightly considered the elite among us, studied Greek in their junior and senior years. Additionally, all CHS students, regardless of their primary academic interests or eventual field of study, had to take four years of Latin. This emphasis on languages represented an educational maxim that if one wanted to learn one's own language, one had to study others. It also represented the traditional Jesuit emphasis on the classics—especially Latin—as the principal focus of the most intellectually challenging and culturally valuable education possible. In his essay "The Jesuit Model of Education," Fr. Michael McMahon quotes the Jesuit historian, Fr. Camille de Rochemonteix, who writes that formative Jesuit educators emphasized Latin "because it was indispensable for the study of philosophy, the crown of a classical education; because it was the idiom of both the Church and of science; because it was the language of the past in religion, literature, philosophy and theology; and because no one thought an education could be liberal without Latin" (16). William J. McGucken, SJ writes of the *Ratio Studiorum*, the establishing document of Jesuit education begun under Claudio Aquaviva in 1581 and finalized at the Collegio Romano in 1599:

> The *Ratio Studiorum* says the purpose of Latin was to teach culture. It wished Latin taught because without it no one can attain the fine appreciation and delight in beautiful things nor be comfortable and at home with them which is the mark of the cultured mind. The *Ratio* wished the pupil to become a master of its expression and its appreciation: to find his reading in Latin books, to express his thoughts in Latin, to talk, to plan, to argue, to dream, to pray, to live in Latin. Mind training, proper formation, was a by-product of Latin teaching. (*The Jesuits and Education*, pp. 163–64)

The immigrant families of Buffalo, some of whom boasted doctors and lawyers but most of whom belonged to what the irascible Irish priest Andrew Greeley called the "white immigrant working class," sent their sons to Canisius, and the Jesuits returned them endowed with a rigorous education steeped in humanities and classical languages. This emphasis on the classics, especially instruction in Latin, for all students regardless of their ethnicity or their parents' educational levels and employment did not seem at all preposterous. For my generation, especially in the aftermath of the European catastrophe, the Jesuits' educational model embodied the basic tenet of rugged American individualism—that one can become whatever one wishes—overlaid with a conviction that knowledge of the classical past—linguistic, historical, literary, philosophical, and cultural— would produce idealistic young men uniquely prepared to restore sanity and decency to the human condition. We would go forth to careers as educators, philosophers, scholars, editors, journalists, historians, physicians, scientists, and lawyers. We would transcend the employment boundaries often faced by our urban, immigrant parents who possessed minimal formal education, little rhetorical skill, and names considered unpronounceable by the Smiths and Joneses who lived in large brick houses in the suburbs. Regardless of our chosen profession, we would embody in our daily lives the Jesuit motto, *Ad majorem dei gloriam* (To the greater glory of God).

A curriculum broadly based in the classics and humanities presumes a set of values about the purpose of education and its intended outcomes. In his brilliant encomium to traditional humanities education, *Toward Freedom and Dignity: The Humanities and the Idea of Humanity,* the medieval scholar O. B. Hardison, Jr. defended the humanities against the attacks he saw coming from supporters of both liberal and vocational education in the early 1970s:

> The demand for simple goals and a pat methodology is a disguised form of the urge of liberal educators and vocationists to put the humanities to some practical use. From the point of view of the humanities themselves, to admit the validity of this impulse is to deny the basic values of humanistic experience—the free play of the mind and its corollary, an expanded sense of the self and its relation to the world. To deny these values would, indeed, be a problem, but it is a problem that disappears as soon as we accept the fact that neither the imagination nor works of imagination can be fitted neatly into the various abstract categories devised to explain them. (p. 26)

An education anchored in classical languages and culture—from Plato, Aristotle, Sophocles and Homer to Caesar and Virgil—expands and invigorates the human imagination. Humanities classes might not produce a technically superior physician, lawyer, teacher, or engineer, but they deepen an individual's sense of his own humanity and broaden his sympathy for and understanding of others, what Hardison terms one's "relation to the world." Northrop Frye, the preeminent literary scholar of my generation, expressed a similar idea in *The Educated Imagination.* The study of literature, he argues, is essential because its language is "associative" and suggests "an identity between the human mind and the world outside it, that identity being what the imagination is chiefly concerned with." (p. 38)

The Jesuit educational philosophy and its humanistic ideals opened our minds far beyond our ethnic neighborhoods. It allowed us to imagine not only a world much different from what our parents had known but also one that we might fashion according to the Christian ideal of loving one's neighbor as one's self. We would go forth with the intellectual talents we had developed and the social virtues we had nurtured. On the cusp of the 1960s, we were poised to share, perhaps unknowingly, in the looming upheavals that would reshape American society in a decade-long quest for racial equality and social justice.

I attended Canisius College from 1961 to 1965. While steeped in Jesuit tradition and values, its curriculum also reflected a genuine openness to the modern world. All students took the required classes in theology and scholastic philosophy, focusing on Thomas Aquinas, and we encountered Christian apologists from Augustine to Karl Barth as well as eclectic thinkers such as Pierre Teilhard de Chardin, whose controversial book *The Phenomenon of Man* appeared in 1957. I studied political science with a radicalized Hungarian professor who had escaped the Nazis and took two semesters of world history that examined the causes of the world wars, totalitarianism, and the Nazi terror. In Fr. Robert O'Brien's philosophy classes, I studied existentialists from Nietzsche and Kierkegaard to Sartre and Camus and American pragmatists such as Charles Pierce, Josiah Royce, and John Dewey.

I fell in love with metaphorical language, majored in English Literature, and read voraciously. Opening each new book was a visceral invitation to words and ideas that fed my relentless hunger for literary knowledge. Our professors were gentlemen scholars who had earned doctoral degrees at prestigious universities like Harvard and Chicago, and we believed that the best of them, such as David Lauerman, Richard Thompson, Charles Brady, and Leslie Warren, had "read everything." We strove to imitate them. They assumed that we could write tolerably well and that we would read, at least once, every play, essay, novel, short story and poem they assigned. We could, and we did. In freshman English, we read masterpieces from Aeschylus to T. S. Eliot, including Shakespeare's *King Lear*, which exploded in my head. We devoured the *Norton Anthology of English Literature* and courses in American literature. We studied Greek tragedy; Hemingway, Fitzgerald, and Faulkner with Richard Thompson; scrutinized W. B. Yeats for hours with Charles Brady; and took every course we could with Leslie Warren: literary criticism and theory from Aristotle to Matthew Arnold to Northrop Frye; Tolstoy's *War and Peace* and critical gems like Isaiah Berlin's *The Hedgehog and the Fox;* and Shakespearean comedy and romance. Professor Warren cracked up reading aloud from *Much Ado about Nothing* and *As You Like It*, spread books all over his desk at the beginning of class, and magically created from them and his obvious love of Shakespeare brilliant insights into the plays.

As Costard says in *Love's Labour's Lost*, this was "remuneration" on a grand scale that propelled me into my teaching and scholarly career and for which I have always been enormously grateful.

Chapter 7:
Religion

The power of religion depends, in the last resort, upon the credibility of the banners it puts in the hands of men as they stand before death, or more accurately, as they walk, inevitably, toward it.
Peter L. Berger, *The Sacred Canopy*, p. 51

Mother was fiercely Catholic. One weekend in the fall of 1971, while she and Father were visiting Gail and me in Madison, she insisted that they had to go to Mass twice on the same day: once for Sunday Mass and once to commemorate some holy day from the previous week during which they had been traveling from Buffalo. Father acquiesced, having decided years before to join the Catholic Church just so Mother would stop nagging him about it. Having completely lost my faith by this time, I was perplexed. Who knew or cared whether my parents went to church twice on the same day? What difference could it possibly make in their spiritual well-being? Did they get extra credit in heaven for attending Holy Mass twice within twenty-four hours? Was there really a God who scrutinized every moment of every day of individual Catholics? What happened to gravity while God was busy counting how many times the world's Catholics went to Mass?

These questions are flippant and facetious, but as I grew older, my struggle with the Catholic Church and religious belief became wrenching. Through at least my middle teens, I clung tenaciously to an all-encompassing spiritual order, a vividly imagined cosmos featuring an omniscient deity whose angelic forces daily battled Satan's army for my wavering soul. I clung to rituals deeply felt and at times terrifying, especially at Easter, and to prayers that, the assignment of paper routes notwithstanding, I believed would be (mostly) answered. I firmly believed that sinful humanity could be forgiven and earn eternal salvation somewhere among the planets. However, despite nearly sixteen years of Catholic education, this cosmic certainty began to crumble in my junior year in college. Reading Greek philosophers, Protestant theologians, and contemporary existentialists, especially Albert Camus and Jean-Paul Sartre, helped this process, but the precipitating event, as for millions of young Catholics in the Sixties, was a conversation with a priest at Canisius College about birth control. A girl I was dating told me that her mother, who was in her mid-forties and had borne several children, refused to use birth control because of her Catholic faith even after she was warned by her doctor that another pregnancy might be fatal. The parish priest had told the girl's parents that since the Church prohibited artificial birth control, they could rely only on the "rhythm method." I was horrified by this assertion. Why risk a woman's life, and possibly leave her children motherless, because some priest told her that God, who never struggled to raise children, didn't want her to use a diaphragm or her husband a condom? I spoke to a theologian, posed a question about this girl's parents using birth control, and was told, as they had been, that the Church outlawed artificial devices. God's will must be obeyed. If God wanted her parents to have another child, they must not interfere with that plan.

"But why would God want the mother to risk dying?" I asked the priest.
"We must not ask such questions. God's ways, Michael, are mysterious."

Mysterious indeed! The crumbling had commenced.

The girl's mother did get pregnant again and, the following August, damn near died giving birth. Near the end of my senior year, the girl's father died in an automobile accident, and while she, her mother, and her siblings survived this terrible emotional shock, my faith did not. What the hell kind of cosmic order was this? Shortly after the funeral, I hurled the Sunday Roman Missal that I had used faithfully for fifteen years into a wastebasket. (Freight cars, prayer books; hurling stuff was my favorite expression of rage.) The whole cosmology and schemata of Christianity—a main component of my psychic need for order—had imploded.

What I lost had been essential to my childhood. The liturgical rituals of the Roman Catholic Church, especially those at Christmas and Easter, anchored the awe and mystery of religion during my early life. The Roman Missal itself was a virtual calendar of my annual journey through the days and weeks of faith. In my copy were two bookmarks: one marking the "Ordinary," the text of the Sunday Mass, and the other the readings from the Old and New Testament for each Sunday of the year. Like a burgeoning textual scholar, when Mass started,

I followed the priest's verbal progression, in Latin and English, through the weekly ritual, and because of my careful attention to every word, I exited the church believing that I had dutifully witnessed the ceremony. Every aspect of the Mass spoke to me of a spiritual realm that only faith could fathom and only ritual could realize.

When I became an altar boy at Saint Aloysius Church, my sense of the spiritualism of the Mass intensified. Serving Mass meant that I was not only reading the scripture but also participating fully in the liturgy. Altar boys were given serving schedules for the Low Mass on weekdays and the High Mass on Sundays. Whether at 7:00 a.m. on weekdays (when I had one of the Dressel brothers deliver my papers) or at 10:00 a.m. on Sundays (when I had to finish the paper route, weather be damned, really early), serving Mass meant arriving at church at least thirty minutes early and even earlier for Sunday High Mass. After donning my red alb and white amice in the small dressing room behind the vestry, I and my co-server prepared the altar. One spread a long white linen cloth across the altar and brought out the handheld bells, while the other lighted two small candles for Low Mass or, for High Mass, six tall candles, three on either side of the central Tabernacle. The candles for High Mass were really high, and even the taller boys had to reach way up with a lighted wick attached to a long pole. This exercise terrified me. Being short, I feared not being able to reach the wicks of the tall candles and thus delaying the start of Mass before a packed church or, worse, accidentally putting out the wick at the top of the pole before I lit all six candles. Either failure would have quickly demoted me to serving only 7:00 Mass on Wednesdays.

After preparing the altar, the servers assisted the priest with his vestments. The priest's dressing was solemn and fascinating. He wore six garments: amice, alb, cincture, maniple, stole, and the richly decorated chasuble, a heavy silk garment that covered him from his shoulders to just below his knees. He donned these vestments in the prescribed order, and each was accompanied by its own kiss of the cloth and, when donning the chasuble, with a prayer that speaks of it as the "yoke of Christ." These vestments, like similar garb in all religions, granted priests the authority to lead ceremonies with words whose power the laity could never know. Kneeling on the bottom steps of that marble altar, serving the richly attired magicians, I fully accepted that premise.

Every moment of the Mass was ritualized. There were times to stand and to kneel in response to the priest's movements and, well before the "modernization" of the Mass by Vatican II, Latin responses to his prayers. High Mass on

Sundays was longer and more complex than the daily Low Mass, and woe to the altar boy who confused the movements and prayers of one with the other! Reprimands for errors were swift and stern. The quintessential ceremony centered on the golden Tabernacle in the middle of the altar that housed the bread and wine for conversion into Christ's body and blood: the Eucharist. Only the priest could open the Tabernacle to retrieve its contents and only at a specified moment in the Mass when chanting the required prayers. The priest's kneeling before the opened Tabernacle, his blessing of the bread and wine, and his elevating them in the golden chalice—the actual moment of transubstantiation—were accompanied by the server on the right side of the altar ringing small bells three times. The bells were themselves symbolic: three gold casings, fastened together at the handle, each containing three small golden balls: three threes in one, the Christian Trinity symbolized in one instrument. The timing and the ringing had to be perfect: not too loudly and not too vigorously. When I was the bell ringer, the syncretism of this moment held me rapt. 'Twas *I* who announced to the congregation this most sacred moment when the wafers and drops of wine became the body and blood of Christ: *Hoc est corpus meus* (This is my body). Facilitating this mystery was ethereal—assuming, of course, that I got the ringing right.

The Christmas and Easter services heightened my feeling of participating in the sacred. Christmas Eve Mass began at midnight, a never-never realm neither night nor day, when I imagined the sacred entering the mundane and transforming not just the interior of a church but also time itself. As intense as the Christmas celebration was, the services of Holy Week, including Holy Thursday, Good Friday, Holy Saturday, and Easter Sunday, were even more enthralling. Attending services these four days created a profound sense of mystery and the power of belief to shape one's imagination. After Mass on Holy Thursday, the priest moved the Eucharist from the Tabernacle to a side altar and then stripped bare the main altar. The stark rituals of the next two days gradually refocused the Christian world from spiritual death to spiritual life. Tenebrae—the darkening of the church on Holy Thursday night, the direct opposite of the exhilarating brightness of Christmas Eve—left me fearful.

On Good Friday, the congregation gathered at noon to pray and contemplate Christ's death. The services included reading the Long Gospel, John's vivid account of Christ's passion and death, followed by a series of prayers for the clergy, the sick, the poor, and those preparing to enter the church, led by the priest and followed by the response, "*Ora pro nobis*" (Pray for us). This simple chant combined all those who sought Christ's intervention on their behalf, and in my imagination, the parishioners' rhythmic response ensured that they would be heard. The Stations of the Cross emphasized Christ's terrible suffering for which, as the nuns insisted in catechism class, even young children were partly responsible. Being told, and for many years believing, that I was partly responsible for this cataclysmic event profoundly affected my childhood through high school. In my mind, every dispute with my parents, every spat with my sisters, every schoolyard fight, every curse of another Buffalo blizzard at 5:00 a.m. ballooned into a sin that sent me scurrying to confession on Saturday afternoons.

On Holy Saturday night, the Paschal Candle was lit in the darkened entrance of the church, and the priest carried it to the front near the communion railing where it burned all night. This ceremony, the movement of light into darkness—Lux et Tenebrae—was rapturous: a single flame against the physical and spiritual darkness. I felt a huge relief when walking into the church on Easter Sunday and embraced the visual and choral splendor of the High Mass. I was again "free of guilt" for whatever sins a child could be convinced plagued his soul.

I marvel now at how quickly I discarded the faith that had been so central to my childhood and, conversely, at my continuing fascination with religious mystery. In Paris in 1972, Gail and I visited Notre-Dame Cathedral, and I was overwhelmed by its sheer magnificence and inherent symbolism. In the cathedral's vast interior, lighted by rainbows streaming through the stained glass windows, I felt a startling humbleness in the house of God. The sheer volume of the astonishing structure resurrected the awe I had felt as a child in a holy place. Looking down the nave of Notre-Dame's white stone toward the Rose Window, I sensed again the spiritual power that faith might evoke in such surroundings, and I longed to believe again in a God whose house this might be. Surely, if simple workmen in the Middle Ages risked their lives on rickety scaffolds building such a structure to their faith, I too could kneel and believe. I recalled John Ormond's poem "Cathedral Builders":

> They climbed on sketchy ladders towards God,
> With winch and pulley hoisted hewn rock into heaven,
> Inhabited sky with hammers, defied gravity,
> Deified stone, took up God's house to meet Him. (lines 1–4)

While teaching in London in 1991, I visited several historic cathedrals in England, including York Minster, Salisbury, Canterbury, and the smaller but elegant

Bath Cathedral. That December, Gail joined me, and we traveled to Italy and visited Saint Peter's Basilica in Rome. As I entered the most renowned of Roman Catholic churches, I anticipated a deeply spiritual experience. The relatively sparse English cathedrals, especially Canterbury and Salisbury, had evoked a profound sense of holiness, but I was shocked by what I encountered in Saint Peter's.

The Basilica is filled with works of art—statues, paintings, monuments, elaborate golden sarcophagi, plaques, engravings, and marvelous sculptures of the High Italian Renaissance. Many of these works are devotional, and many are beautifully executed, including Michelangelo's magnificent *Pieta* and Bernini's splendid *Altar of the Chair of Saint Peter*. The predominant sensation is of a church devoted to the works of man, and to gold, rather than to a humble worship of God. The floor plan numbers eighty items, including twenty-six monuments to popes (hardly the humble descendants of Saint Peter) and twenty-five altars. Bernini's gigantic Baroque altar is a testament to the amount of money the Catholic Church is willing to spend on ornament, not to the littleness of man in God's house.

After walking around the Basilica for an hour, I said to Gail, "I could never worship in this church." As we left, I was crying.

My tours through the renowned churches of Paris, England, and Rome were not about different approaches to cathedral architecture—Italian Baroque versus English plain style—or vastly different ideas about how to worship God. Notre-Dame and especially Canterbury and Salisbury rekindled the awe and solemnity I felt in church as a child, whereas Saint Peter's Basilica evoked Mammon. The vast interior of Saint Peter's is resplendent with the most elaborate and expensive artistic works money could buy. If what mattered to the hierarchy of the Catholic Church was the sheer magnificence of its central place of worship, how could such grandeur house the poor, clothe the naked, and feed the hungry? Had not Christ thrown the moneychangers out of the Temple and told his followers not to care for the clothes they wore? Why did popes prance about wearing richly embroidered vestments and demand golden memorials to their worldly splendor?

The simplicity of my childhood faith, shrouded in mystery and awe, was shattered, but that faith was also hopelessly naïve in the ways of the world. I know this. Roman Catholic bishops and cardinals want to be known as men of the world in their sartorial finery, but given where my sense of and immersion in Roman Catholicism had started, my fall from belief—perhaps from grace as well—was inevitable. Such was the hold of faith and its attendant rituals that returning to that childhood religion became impossible. Having become a cynic, perhaps now I know what Christ meant when he said, "We must become as children again to enter the kingdom of heaven."

I seldom attend religious services now, and when I do, I attend a Protestant church. The unadorned simplicity of Saint Mark's Cathedral in Seattle, the seat of the Episcopal diocese, reminds me of Salisbury and Canterbury. The Catholic bishop of Seattle recently authorized millions for extensive renovations to Saint James Cathedral, the seat of the Catholic diocese. Its interior, like Saint Peter's, now shimmers. The bishop wanted a more glorious performance space for religious concerts and ceremonies performed there every year, but I cannot but wonder how such ostentatious renovations serve doing unto others as we would have them do unto us. Saint James Cathedral seems less a church, a place of worship, and more a theatre or place of entertainment. Where in such lavish expenditures is the humbleness that enables us to see ourselves in others, as Christ asked of us?

I still listen frequently to religious choral works—Allegri's stunning *Miserere,* Rachmaninoff's *Vespers,* J. S. Bach's *Mass in B Minor* and *Magnificat, and* Mozart's *Requiem.* These latter works enthrall me. Mozart writes stunning choral crescendos in the third movement, *Dies Irae* (Days of Wrath), and in the final movement, *Lux Aeterna* (Light Eternal) that stress the extremes of religious experience: despair and hope. An explosive crescendo in the fourth movement of Bach's *Magnificat* proclaims the Virgin Mary "blessed" and boldly asserts all generations' belief in miracle. Mozart and Bach transport me to a simpler time in a parish church, to the paschal candle procession on Holy Saturday night and the still moments before Midnight Mass, when the awe and mystery of faith were central to my life. Still, I do not believe or, stubbornly, refuse to believe.

Across the street from the small college on High Street Kensington in London where I taught in the fall of 1991 stands the venerable Saint Mary Abbott's Church. It was damaged by bombs in World War II and, typical of London, is located half a block from a pub, The Catherine Wheel. One day after lunch, late in the term, I ventured into the church and sat down in a pew next to the central aisle.

> Inside this graying church
> Of ancient silence,
> Adjacent rushed insanity
> Of High Street Kensington,
> A somber, crimson cat

Prowls the aisle,

Looking for mice, or lost souls.

One look, he knows,

And leaps into my seat.

I wrote these lines later that evening. They are true; the cat knew.

Parce mihi Domine, nihil enim sunt dies mei (Spare me, Lord, for my days are truly as nothing). Unbidden, this communion motet still haunts my memory.

Chapter 8:
"Ah, the Hell with It!"

—m—

This was the favorite expression of my Uncle Frank, Father's oldest brother, who from among the mélange of relatives sewn into the fabric of my life on Highgate emerges irresistibly in my memory.

Frank was a gruff, hard-drinking, hard-driving, jovial, impatient, cantankerous Ukrainian-Polish bear of a man who swerved in and out of my childhood and became a second father to me. Despite significant differences in their personalities, Father and Frank were always close, not only in age—just a year apart—but also in mutual interests: tools, tinkering with machines, especially cars, and baseball. They spent endless hours together, and once I was old enough to enter their shared, exclusively masculine world, I learned to treasure Uncle Frank as a source of endless joy.

Frank was loud. His sentences roared to their conclusion, as if sheer volume guaranteed the truth of what he said. He was often overbearing, and his enthusiasm for whatever he was discussing could seem belligerent, especially to people who did not know him well. He didn't care what people thought about him, and his aggressive tone, even with strangers, often turned a social event into a train wreck. Although he and his wife, Olga, lived together for twenty-nine years, I fear that she suffered emotionally from his confrontational approach to everyone and everything around him. Despite his explosive personality, he genuinely cared about his siblings, most of his in-laws, and his nephew and nieces. He was quintessentially Buffalonian: endearing in direct proportion to his gruffness.

Since Mother did not like quiet people, Frank was her favorite brother-in-law. During family gatherings, she and Frank never talked to each other: they *yelled* at each other! A party with Frank and Olga, at our house or theirs, was an endless din. If Mother had married Frank instead of my quiet, peace-loving father, their children would have been deaf by age five. Frank would get a few under his belt and say something that Mother considered foolhardy or obnoxious, and they'd be at each other for the rest of the evening. Father chimed in whenever he could, but to be heard, he yelled, and then Frank launched into diatribes aimed at his brother, whom he always called Junior. Before long, the rafters rang with relentless shouting at ever-increasing decibels.

Mother's favorite story about Frank, which she told repeatedly, involved his false teeth and Rusty, his gregarious cocker spaniel. Frank watched TV late into the night and always removed his false teeth and placed them on a small plate on a table next to his chair. One Saturday, Frank forgot to take his dentures back into the bathroom before going to bed, and the next morning he spent several minutes looking for them. When Olga suggested that he might have left them on the table next to his chair, he went to the chair and found his mangled dentures on the floor. Rusty had jumped onto the chair, grabbed the dentures, and, thinking they were bones, chewed them. Olga told us later that Frank raged for hours as only he could about the goddamn dog, while she calmly reminded him who had left them on the table. Mother adored the absurd humor of this story, and whenever she thought she was losing an argument to Frank and really wanted to get his goat, she reminded him about the night Rusty chewed his teeth.

> "Hey Frank, when are you going to start feeding Rusty enough food? The poor thing must be awfully hungry if he's eating dentures. They can't be too good for him."
> "Hey Irish, will you shut the hell up about that damn dog? How the hell was I to know he would try to eat the lousy dentures? For Christ's sake, they musta tasted terrible. Stupid mutt!"
> "Want me to call you tonight to remind you to take your dentures into the bathroom? Want to take some of Brandy's food home with you? We've got plenty."
> "Junior, for Christ's sake will you pour Mary another drink and tell her to lay off my teeth?"
> "Ha! Gotcha!"

Mother and Frank entertained themselves and a host of relatives for hours yelling at each other, igniting raucous, bombastic festivity as only they could. My parents didn't need TV or movies for entertainment; they just had a party and invited Frank.

Frank was an excellent professional printer, and for many years, he worked for a commercial press in Buffalo. He was also quite adventurous. In the mid-Fifties he quit the printing business and bought a Mobil station at 470 East Delavan Avenue at Fillmore; it became Shurgot's Service Station. Because of his mechanical skills and his genial, if gruff, personality, he had many customers for both gasoline and auto repairs who valued his skills and the generally hospitable, male-only atmosphere that he maintained at the station. Frank made a decent living there for many years, at least into the early 1960s. For what seems like a thousand Saturdays, Shurgot's Service Station was a delightful haven for Father and me.

We arrived around 9:00 a.m. Father parked to the left of the service bay entrance so that he would not block any of the cars that Frank worked on during the day. In the center of the large apron in front of the service bays were the twin gas pumps, and rising between them was a tall, metal pole topped by the Mobil Oil Company's logo: a dark-blue winged horse and the word "Mobil" in huge, red-and-blue letters against a white background. Very patriotic! I marveled at that impressive sign; it symbolized my uncle's command of his station. When Father and I walked into the station, Frank hollered, "Hello, Junior! Whadda ya know?" and greeted me with "Hey kid, are you behavin' yourself, because if you ain't, you know what you'll get!" Frank took it upon himself to help my father raise me, possibly because he realized that his son Craig was nearly unmanageable, and he wanted to prevent his nephew from going astray.

Frank's constant companion at his station was a large, purebred German Shepherd named Captain—Cap for short. Cap lived at the station and guarded the place every night after Frank left for home. Cap was gentle to those he knew, including Father and me, and let us pet him as soon as he recognized us. I imagined that he was a fierce obstacle to anyone who ventured anywhere near the station after Frank closed it, much less tried to rob the place. Just his growl was intimidating! Cap slept on a rug near the cash register every night, was overjoyed to see Frank every morning, and delighted with extra company on Saturdays.

Saturdays at Frank's station were deliciously chaotic. Given his location at a busy intersection, he sold a lot of gas. Because he spent Saturdays buried in car engines or rolling under them on a cart, cussing constantly from the inner sanctum of the service bays, Craig, Father and I ran the pumping business. Father manned the till with Cap at his side, whose presence discouraged anyone from contesting his bill. Craig and I pumped the gas, which I am sure today would violate child labor laws, but it was an immense thrill for a kid. Customers pulled up to the pump, and, trying to imitate Frank, Craig and I firmly inquired, "Regular or high-tech? How much?" Exuding manly authority, we removed the gas cap, inserted the hose into the tank, monitored the flow of gas, and stopped at the precise amount that the customer requested. If the customer trusted us with his payment, walking back to the station with dollar bills in our hand solidified our feeling of acceptance into this masculine world of high finance and complex mechanics, especially if we had to make change at the till. Lest we forget where we were, every half hour Frank yelled from under a hood, "How's it goin', Junior?" as a way of reminding us who was boss.

Because he was a crack mechanic, by 10:00 a.m. the station was crammed with customers. Frank refused to make appointments, a failure in business etiquette and common sense that my eminently practical father never understood. Drivers who wanted something fixed immediately quickly filled the apron in front of the service stalls, while other guys jockeyed around the parked cars trying to get to the gas pumps. Watching this circus, Dad tried every Saturday to convince Frank that he could make more money if he just got organized.

> "Frank, when the hell are you going to start making appointments? I've told you this a dozen times. Look at this place. How can you keep track of who was first? You need a secretary at this place on Saturdays!"
> "Junior, I just remember, that's all. I don't need any damn appointments, and I sure as hell don't want a secretary. I don't want a dame in here on a Saturday when I'm tryin' to work. How could I afford a secretary? The hell with that idea!"

Variations of this conversation careened around the station all morning, eventually joined by customers who, while not necessarily irate at Frank, become impatient.

> "Hey Frank, I got here at nine thirty. I thought ya'd need lots of time to figure out that rattle, and them damn brakes in the back are squealing again. When do ya figure you'll get at 'em? I ain't got all day. My old lady says she needs the car by one."
> "Yeah yeah, I heard ya. This Chrysler just needs an oil change. I'll get it outta here quick."
> "Yeah sure, but Frank, I was here ahead of that guy. I told ya I got here early so's you could work on my car right away in case it needs a lotta work. Like I says,

my wife says she needs the car by one, and I don't want no fuckin' grief today. I
got enough crap on my mind as it is."
  "Ah shit, Joe, just give me a few more minutes, will ya? Have some more
coffee, why don't ya?"

Frank kept a coffee pot and cups on a table just inside the front door, and
customers stood around sipping coffee from cups that hadn't been rinsed, let
alone washed, in years. As he bustled in and out of the service area, Frank carried
on noisy conversations with everyone in his shop. They were mostly returning
customers whom he knew well. When the coffee ran out or became too rancid
(I swear he never cleaned that pot either), Frank handed around a metal slug that
customers inserted into his red-and-white Coca-Cola dispenser, thus getting
free Cokes. I can't imagine how much money he lost on that Coke machine, but
he probably figured that the free drinks would keep customers returning. Dad
could not understand Frank's liberal attitude toward refreshments.

  "Frank, you're losing too damn much money on that Coke machine. Why don't
  you charge people for those bottles?'
  "Ah, Junior, it's only a couple bucks. The hell with it!"

Across the street from Frank's station, at 484 East Delavan, was a bar called
Strinka's. Whether or not Frank bought that Mobil station, as opposed to another
one somewhere else, because of its proximity to a grog shop, I do not know. I
do know that the owner, a guy my father and Frank called "Bud," opened early
on Saturdays because he knew that Frank would have lots of customers. Strinka's
became a convenient annex to Frank's station, serving as a second waiting room
for customers when the station got too crowded. As Frank's repairs stretched
into midafternoon, and his customers, tired of rank coffee and sugary Cokes,
became hungry and thirsty, they drifted across the street where they ate meatball
and salami sandwiches on rye and drank whisky or beer while watching a ball-
game on TV. The later Frank worked on cars, the more I smelled whisky on the
customers' breath, and by late afternoon, guys whose cars required major work
returned from the bar well-oiled themselves. Presumably they had enough cash
left to pay their repair bill, this being long before credit cards.
  When gas sales finally slowed around 4:00 p.m. and Frank had completed
most of the repair jobs, he and Father decided it was their time for libations. Frank

put a hand-lettered sign on top of the gas pump that read "Leave money inside," left Cap in the office chained to the table by the cash register, and we all headed for Strinka's. Bud let me and Craig sit at the bar and have a root beer while my dad and Frank imbibed shots or beer and chatted with Bud about baseball, football, the price of gas, their wives' cooking and wardrobe, and lake-effect snow. Frank followed this routine every Saturday afternoon, and that he trusted his customers to leave their gas money next to the till is absolutely astonishing to me. Father berated Frank for this routine ("For Christ's sake Frank, one of these days some-body's going to walk in there and steal the whole cash register!") but to no avail. Frank always insisted that "Nobody's gonna steal one damn nickel with Cap sittin' there!" Still, one wonders at his motivation. Trustworthiness? Naiveté? "The hell with it!"? All three? Cap's presence next to the table encouraged honesty—Cap was huge, and customers never approached the cash register, just left money on the table. While Frank knew many of his regular customers, I still cannot believe that when we returned to the station an hour or two later, he actually found cash on the table. Did Frank lose money while drinking at Strinka's? I will never know, nor did he, but ultimately, it does not matter.

What matters is that nothing as mundane as worrying about money inter-fered with Frank's ramshackle journey through life. Today no one in his right mind would dare run a business the way Frank ran that station, but I suppose that his nonchalant approach reflected a far more trusting urban environment than is possible today in any American city. He can't have done too badly. He made enough money at that station to retire with a decent pension, so he could not have lost too much money on stolen fuel or free Cokes. Besides, Cap had damn good vision and an excellent memory. He knew a potential thief when he saw one.

The remarkable fact about this usual Saturday schedule was that if Father wanted Frank to work on his car, as happened frequently with our many clunk-ers, Frank began only *after* returning from Strinka's, often as late as five or six. Accompanied by garrulous cussing about the wrecks that his brother begged him to keep running, Frank, well lubricated himself, dove under the hood and worked for sometimes an hour or two on another interminable mechanical problem. One would think that during these late afternoon/early evening ses-sions Frank's mechanical aptitude would have faded. Not so. The miracle was not that for all those years he kept Father's cars running *in spite of* his visits to Strinka's but probably *because of* them! No completely sober mechanic would have agreed to work on Dad's cars, and only a somewhat inebriated genius could keep them all running.

Besides their mutual interest in banging around cars, Father and Frank shared another passion common to many immigrant families: baseball. Had they lived in a city with a major league baseball team, they would have attended many games. Living in Buffalo, they had to be content with the AAA Buffalo Bisons, a minor league affiliate of the Cleveland Indians, whose games they attended occasionally. Watching the Bisons, however, wasn't enough to satisfy their love of the game. Whenever they got together at Frank's station, at Strinka's, or at a family gathering at Grandma Shurgot's, baseball often animated their conversation. Given Frank's boisterous approach to every subject, and his and Father's radically different views of their favorite New York teams, their conversations about baseball were loud, virulent, and immensely entertaining. My most vivid memories of their incessant arguments about New York baseball emanate from many hilarious Sunday symposia held around our kitchen table on Highgate.

Frank was audacious in his own charming way and completely oblivious to what others thought of his antics. He said, did, and wore whatever he damn well pleased and the devil take the hindmost. On those Sunday mornings when Frank came to our house to listen with Father to Yankee baseball narrated sonorously by Mel Allen, he always wore the same uniform: brown slippers, green bathrobe, and striped cotton pajamas. Frank believed that if his bedroom attire was suitable for sleeping, it was suitable for listening to a ball game. Without calling ahead, he drove over and parked in our driveway, figuring that since the baseball season had begun, Father was expecting him. About 11:45, when our fine Christian neighbors, just returned from church, were piously preparing for a day of family togetherness in their backyards, Frank barreled into the house and bellowed, "Hey Junior, whadda ya know?" Anticipating a festive afternoon, he carried a bottle of whiskey in his right hand. Early in the season, the whiskey was usually Canadian Club, but in June or July, especially if the Yankees were winning, Frank brought Four Roses, which he considered superior. During my childhood, New York had three major league teams: the Yankees, the Giants, and the Brooklyn Dodgers. Ever the successful entrepreneur, Frank adored the Yankees and despised not just the Dodgers and Giants but the whole National League. "They're all lousy teams there," he'd flatly declare. "No guts!"

My father, whose spotty employment history in Buffalo made him appreciate underdogs, loved the Dodgers, although for reasons I never understood he was indifferent to the Giants. I am sure, however, that he *hated* the Yankees. They won too often—single games, doubleheaders, pennants, and the World Series. For this constant success, my father never forgave them. No amount of whiskey could ameliorate this basic dispute between my father and uncle about the Dodgers and the Yankees.

As the season progressed and the pennant races (and the weather) heated up, the whiskey intensified their discord.

Sunday games began at 1:00 p.m. After Frank planted himself in our kitchen and opened the bottle, he and Father sipped whiskey for about an hour before game time, and during the sipping, they debated incessantly the previous week's games and the league standings. As the Yankees and the Dodgers often led the American and National Leagues in the era of "Willie, Mickey, and the Duke" (the Giants' Willie Mays, the Yankees' Mickey Mantle, and the Dodgers' Duke Snider, all center fielders), there was little reason to dispute the standings. Father and Frank did anyway. Being equally stubborn, they argued the scores of recent games and league standings without consulting the sports section of the *Courier-Express* that, strewn across the living room floor twenty feet away, recapped the week's games. They bickered over batting averages, pitching records, and home run and runs-batted-in stats without consulting the sports pages. They also squabbled about the teams' respective managers: Casey Stengel of the Yankees and Charlie Dressen of the Dodgers. By this time, each had had a few sips, and as Father hated Stengel and Frank thought Dressen a loud-mouth imbecile, this discourse became animated.

"Frank, I'm tellin' you, Stengel is a clown. He wins so damn many games only because the Yankees buy him the best possible team. Any fool could manage the Yankees to a World Series title."
"Ah bullshit, Junior. Casey is a genius. You just can't understand how important a good manager is. You don't know what the hell you're talkin' about!"
"Bullshit yourself! All Stengel has to do is look down his bench and wave any jerk up to the plate and he'll get a hit."
"Yeah, and Dodger pitchers are so bad, blind men could hit them."

On and on it went until the beginning of the game, when Mel Allen's invocation to Yankee baseball—"Brought to you by Ballantine Ale. Ask the man for Ballantine wherever you see the three ring sign: purity, body, flavor!"—demanded our attention.

For this history of baseball on Highgate, it is necessary to understand that besides disparaging Casey Stengel, my father detested Mel Allen. He called him "Meathead." I never knew the origin of this moniker, but Father's complaint about Allen was that he didn't just narrate the games. He deliberately favored the Yankees and made them sound superior or, if they were losing, the victims of bad luck, lousy umpiring, or both. Frank, being a Yankee fan, assumed that Allen was always right. Thus, from virtually the first pitch of the game, Father and Frank battled about whatever Allen said, be it a disputed smash down the left field line—fair or foul?—or a called third strike against Yogi Berra, the best bad-ball-hitter in baseball.

As the innings—and the whiskey consumption—progressed, Allen's broadcast, the actual oral history of that Sunday's game, became increasingly contentious. A line drive might be called foul by an umpire, and if Allen so much as hinted that it "looked fair," Father immediately accused him of favoritism and conjured a whole catalog of transgressions from previous broadcasts. Sitting at the kitchen table, I was amazed at my father's memory.

"How the hell can Meathead tell whether it's fair or foul? He can't see a damn thing from where he's sitting. He's always claiming the Yankee hits are fair even when they're foul by ten feet. That one was foul by at least six feet."
"How do you know he can't see anything? You ever been to Yankee Stadium! You got any idea where the press box is? What the hell do you know, Junior? How do you know it was foul anyway? You're not there. He just said it looked fair, that's all."

When Mantle homered, as he often did, Frank chortled about "natural talent" and how many rows deep in right field the ball landed, while Father described the same homer as a lucky fly ball hit into a tail wind.

"The pitcher shoulda been lifted two innings ago. He's tired."
"How do you know he's tired, Junior?"
"He pitched just four days ago."
"No he didn't. Detroit has a five-man rotation. He pitched last Tuesday."
"Horseshit! He pitched Wednesday. The Tigers have a four-man rotation."
"He's tired. His arm is shot. Detroit always overuses their pitchers. He shoulda been lifted before he pitched to Mantle."

"He ain't tired. Mantle can hit anybody. Rest don't matter. Mantle hit his best fastball. Mantle can hit anybody's fastball."

"How the hell do you know it was his best fastball? You don't even know what he threw at Mantle."

"Allen said it was a fastball."

"Allen couldn't tell a fastball from a goddamn watermelon."

"Ah, bullshit. Damn it, Junior, have another shot!"

Pitching changes were especially vulnerable to historical revision. Stengel's decision to lift a starting pitcher late in the game, and deeper into the Canadian Club or Four Roses, inevitably invoked my father's derision. Allen always insisted that Stengel's decisions were "prudent," even if the Yankees lost. Clutch hitting by Detroit, Cleveland, Chicago or Boston was always, according to Allen, accidental. Father insisted that Stengel not only could not handle pitchers but also did not have to.

"Ford can't pitch worth a damn. He's lucky he's got any victories at all. He wins because the Yankees always get him at least ten runs. Besides, he always pitches against lousy hitting teams, Boston or the White Sox. If Stengel didn't have six relievers to put in, Ford wouldn't win a game all year. He never finishes."

"Now what the hell are you talking about, Junior? Ford's got a great arm. He's already won twelve games this season. He never needs bullpen help. Look at his stats."

"The hell with the stats. He's lucky, I tell ya, and Meathead just makes up those figures. He doesn't know what Ford's ERA is or anybody else's for that matter. Nobody else in the American League can hit, that's all. The Yankees just buy all the good talent and lock it up. Damn it! Any pitcher on the Yankees can win. Stengel doesn't even know what his pitching rotation is. He just sends out to the mound whoever happens to show up that day, whoever isn't hung over. Reynolds, Raschi, Lopat, Spahn, Dizzy Dean. It doesn't matter."

"Spahn don't pitch for the Yankees! He's with the Braves! And Dean is on television! He ain't pitching anymore! He's retired. Holy shit! You really don't know what the hell you're talkin' about. You don't know nothin' about baseball anyway. What are you sayin'? Gimme me that bottle!"

About four o'clock, with Yogi Berra's, Mickey Mantle's or Hank Bauer's ninth-inning blast into the bleachers having secured another Yankee victory, Frank and my despondent father tipped the bottle for a final shot, although for different reasons. While our neighbors completed their backyard family pic-nics, complete with Kool-Aid, peanut butter and jelly sandwiches, and choco-late chip cookies, Dad and Frank vehemently defended their final version of the day's events at Yankee Stadium. Given Buffalo's sultry summers, this col-loquy occurred with the kitchen windows wide open, so our neighbors, much against their will, heard the spicy language of this irreverent debate. Only when Mel "Meathead" Allen gave all the scores from the day's games and sum-marized their effects on the standings in the American and National Leagues, and the last drops of whiskey were consumed, did these symposia end with Allen's urging his listeners to look for the three-ring sign and "ask the man for Ballantine."

Mother disparaged Frank's contentious Sunday visits, commencing as they always did so soon after Mass at Saint Aloysius, but I adored them. Sitting at the kitchen table with my dad and Frank, I entered, as I did at Shurgot's Service Station, another segment of the adult male world where a boy's game became a man's obsession. As a burgeoning fan, I learned from these Sunday colloquies that the history of baseball is not written in sports pages. Baseball's essential history is a spontaneous, evanescent, oral mythology that, like all mythologies, tells us in its tale much about its teller. Yankee fans, like my Uncle Frank, still revel in Billy Martin's circus catch of Jackie Robinson's pop fly to short right field in the seventh inning of the seventh game of the 1952 World Series. Dodger fans, like my father, still insist that Martin (whom Roger Kahn dubbed "the raucous banana-nose from Berkeley" [p. 93]) was lucky. Take your pick; choose your history.

The personal histories of my uncle and father ended within two years of each other. Each died of pancreatic cancer in his mid-Sixties: Frank in October 1973 and Father in August 1975. Tales outlive their tellers, however, and mem-ory endures. I do not now search for the history of baseball in the sports section of *The Seattle Times*. Rather, the game's history drifts toward my memory from an open window on a sultry Sunday in Buffalo, where Mel Allen begins anew the most cherished cacophony of my childhood. In that memory, Father and Uncle Frank forever engage their garrulous debates about the Yankees and the Dodgers.

Frank careened through life, exasperated everyone, and, as his favorite expression and unorthodox management style indicated, didn't care about tomorrow or others' opinions of him—"Ah, the hell with it." What mattered was today and how he spent it, and if you weren't willing to go along for the ride, you had better get out of his way. His abundant energy and frenetic spirit were magnetic, and time spent with him, at the station or around our kitchen table, was sheer delight.

CHAPTER 9:
CRUISIN'

—⋙—

In the 1950s and 1960s, the heyday of the American automobile, every kid had a love affair with cars, preferably his own but also—as in my case—his friends' cars. On rare occasions he might also covet his girlfriend's car but never—absolutely never—his parents' car. This period produced some classics: the 1957 Chevy Impala with sweeping rear fins, the roaring Pontiac Trans-Am convertible with a 404 hp engine, the Plymouth Fury that was so powerful that even state troopers drove them, the Oldsmobile Cutlass with the massive front grill, and Ford's early models of the two-seater Mustang and Thunderbird. These cars were fast, wasteful, polluting, and ridiculously dangerous. Never mind mandatory head rests, seat belts, or interiors designed to minimize serious injuries. Air bags? Never dreamed of in a carmaker's philosophy. Style and muscle mattered, nothing else.

Because Paul Fiutak, Joe Rautenstrauch, Larry Riester, George Singleton, Lenny Wiltburger, Kevin Reyner, and I turned eighteen within a few months of each other, and we took driver's education courses in our junior year of high school, we got our driver's licenses and became old enough to drink legally during our senior year in high school. This combination of a license and car at seventeen, and legal drinking at eighteen, was potentially deadly, and the Fed's raising the drinking age to twenty-one many years later undoubtedly resulted from too many fatal accidents involving drunk eighteen -year-old drivers. Before the government changed the rules, we had a hell of a good time.

Friday was barhopping and girl-chasing night, and, depending on the size of our contingent, we ventured forth in Paul's and/or Larry's classy chariots. Larry had a '57 Ford convertible that, with the top down, allowed us to master the cool "wind in your hair" pseudo-Elvis effect while slithering through traffic on pulsating summer evenings. Paul's first car was a fully loaded, 1956 Olds

88 two-door hardtop with "Glass Pac" mufflers that rumbled gloriously when he downshifted, a booming radio, a freight horn for terrifying little old ladies meandering around town, a wolf whistle to attract pretty girls, especially on the beach, and fuzzy golden rugs. A real babe car!

We patronized bars all over town, including Strinka's (my Father's and Uncle Frank's Saturday hangout), and Maxl's, a German place at Main and Ferry where we became known as regulars. At both places, we could get beer—cheap and cold—served in pitchers until three in the morning, an hour after the usual closing time for Buffalo's bars. We frequented Gleason's and the Park Meadow (aka "the PM") in the upscale Delaware Park neighborhood where we tried to pick up nursing students from Canisius College and education majors from Buffalo State Teachers College. We pursued nurses and teachers because, we said, they were especially intelligent, but given that we were eighteen, perhaps only their looks really mattered, especially in a crowded bar on a Friday night. Other favorite haunts included the Hotel Worth on Main Street, the Rendezvous Room, and, closer to home (we loved this irony), The Library and Mann's 300 Club on Bailey near Highgate.

On summer weekends, we ventured to some of the finer watering holes in South Buffalo along the lake shore. Favorites included Bill Miller's Bar and South Shore Inn, but *the* place for hanging out was Lerczak's. Because drinks were cheap and girls were plentiful, it was always packed and jubilant. The drive back, unless we crashed on someone's couch in a lakeside cottage, was always precarious, and Paul's favorite Lerczak's story involves me at the wheel, six guys crowded into our '64 Chevy II (hardly a muscle car), and a benevolent New York State Trooper. Paul claims that this night I consumed "one of every drink in the joint," and while driving home with a car full of rollicking drunks, I got pulled over, probably for speeding and/or reckless driving. Everyone was certain that I would go to jail and they would have to hitch a ride back to Buffalo, but I had the presence of mind to appear calm as I explained to the trooper that I was fine and anxious to get home. The trooper said, "Well, we will follow you to the county line, and we don't want to see you back here ever again." I drove off slowly and carefully while the guys exploded in laughter. I have no memory of that night, but I vaguely remember one night driving the wrong way up a New York State Thruway exit ramp. Cruisin' in the early Sixties could be dangerous. Lucky (stupid) me! Don't try this at home! (Gail insists that my guardian angel must have retired early from exhaustion.)

Although Buffalo neighborhoods were rigidly segregated, several bars and clubs featured jazz and blues where whites and blacks, drawn primarily by the music, mingled freely. Our favorite was Dubel's, near Canisius College south of Humboldt Parkway. Others, like Lulubelle's, Johnny's Ellicott Grill at Ellicott and Genesee, and The Buena Vista Club on Hertel Avenue, offered local talent, and many of the musicians could be heard on radio station WUFO, which featured blues and jazz 24-7. While the patrons at these clubs, as well as the bouncers who checked our IDs, were primarily black, everyone came to enjoy the music, and these clubs encouraged racial mingling as few other institutions in Buffalo did. As long as we paid the cover charge and bought enough beer, we were welcome.

By my late teens, having purchased several jazz albums by Miles Davis, Sonny Rollins, J. J. Johnson, the Modern Jazz Quartet, and John Coltrane, and having spent many nights at home listening to WUFO's soulful sounds, I felt comfortable in these clubs, despite being a distinct minority. These clubs introduced us, a bunch of guys from all-white neighborhoods, to a principal ingredient of African American culture in Buffalo. Like many of the bars we frequented, especially Strinka's and Maxl's, these clubs were open well past midnight, and they provided us with a sense of adventure and daring that took us far from our comfortable white world.

After barhopping, we were hungry, so on our way home we stopped at a wholesale doughnut shop called Freddie's at the corner of Main and Michigan that supplied doughnuts and pastries to Buffalo restaurants and was open all night. We bought a mixed dozen of glazed, peanut-covered, chocolate cream puff, and lemon custard doughnuts and devoured them. We theorized that the doughnuts absorbed the beer and kept us sober, which may have been true, but the fact that we didn't vomit all the way back to northeast Buffalo is incredible. Our guts must have become accustomed to this onslaught of beer, sugar, and grease. The final stop of these gallant forays was an all-night diner called Deco's somewhere on Main Street where we usually landed around two in the morning. Because by this time most of us were plastered—Paul's expression for this forlorn condition was "clobbed on your ear"—our noisy cussing at the lousy food and cold coffee often got our collective butts booted out.

Friday nights also meant dances at the Catholic high schools, usually sponsored by the senior class. These affairs were called "hops" (as in Danny & The Juniors' "At the Hop"). Before entering, we received a stamp on the back of our hands that was read under a special blue light so that we could go out for a cigarette or beer and get back into the dance. The music was rock n' roll 45 rpm records piped into a large auditorium that doubled as a basketball court and/ or assembly hall and had the intimacy of a hospital emergency room. Several high schools sponsored these mixers, including Bishop Fallon on Main Street, Saint Joe's in Kenmore, Canisius on Delaware Avenue, and occasionally Nardin Academy, an expensive, private girls' school across the street from Canisius.

Although the dances were called hops or mixers, neither label was accurate. While there was some hopping around by a few dancers during the fast numbers, there wasn't much mixing; they were, in fact, sterile. The girls wore dresses—never slacks—and the boys wore shirts, jackets, and ties. For most of the evening, the guys lined up on one side of the auditorium and the girls on the other, and they stared at each other across the empty space while eminently danceable music blared from the loudspeakers. The guys pretended that they were looking for just the right girl to ask for a dance, and the girls stood around in packs of four or five, terrified that some guy would ask them to dance a slow one because their mothers had warned them not to let boys dance too closely. Dancing a fast number could be dangerous if the girl's breasts bounced around as she jitterbugged across the floor and tried to avoid eye contact lest she send an inviting message to her partner, who wasn't watching her eyes anyway. This was the *early* Sixties, and we were all such good Catholic boys and girls that *everybody* was a vigilant virgin and determined to remain so until the wedding night. So not much mixing, and certainly no bumping or grinding.

These dances now seem straight out of Orwell's *1984*. Administrators and teachers at these Catholic schools took the educational principle *in loco parentis* (in place of the parents) seriously. While the students were at school, they were in the capable hands of the faculty and staff that acted in the place of the parents and thus bore a moral responsibility to protect their charges from physical or moral danger. At the Canisius and Nardin mixers, this principle was taken to extremes. All evening, the priests at Canisius and nuns at Nardin, like so many telescreens, peered at their charges from seats in the auditorium. If a couple danced too many consecutive slow ones, gradually moving their bodies closer together in ever-tighter circles, a priest or nun would leap up from the seats and rush to the dance floor, determined to protect the innocent couple from any closer contact and the lewd thoughts that might percolate in their young minds. The roving clergy constituted an anti-sex league, and we were all unsuspecting

Winstons and Julias being watched constantly. No guys were allowed to even imagine what girls' bodies *really* looked like under their many layers of clothing.

We spent long summer afternoons, usually in Larry's convertible or Paul's hot Olds, cruisin' up and down the white sands of Sherkston and Elco Beaches on the Canadian side of Lake Erie. Here was a haven for horny teenagers where there were no roving field marshals from the anti-sex league and daring girls wore as little as possible. We left early on a Saturday or Sunday morning and, because there was an admission fee and my friends' cars had large trunks, we pulled off the road about a mile from the entrance and piled two or three guys into the trunk in order to outwit the fee collector. We usually eluded detection and drove a half mile around a bend toward the lake before stopping to free the illegal aliens from their bumping, suffocating cage. Only occasionally when some bastard living along the road saw us get into the trunk and called the cops did we get caught, and then we paid an extra fee for trying to sneak in, or we headed home. As the line of cars entering the beach complex was often long, the possibility loomed that the guys in the trunk could be asphyxiated by the exhaust fumes as Paul's or Larry's car crawled toward the toll booth, but we never considered this danger. What mattered was outwitting the poor sap collecting the fee and having more money for Molson's Export Ale at the concession stand.

On Saturday and Sunday afternoons, Sherkston and Elco were packed. People arrived as early as 9:00 a.m., claimed a spot, and parked facing the water so they could sit on the hoods of their cars and watch the beautiful people of the opposite sex saunter down the sands. Guys threw footballs around in the shallow water, showing off their biceps and making athletic dives for touchdowns. Girls in revealing bikinis dashed into the lake just far enough to say they had "gone swimming" and then spent the rest of the day lying on their tummies and backs acquiring the de rigueur tan. The daring girls unhooked the top of their bikini while lying on their stomachs, sending sexually crazed pseudo-athletes into a frenzy at the sight of a girl's naked back.

With their classy cars, guys and girls drove slowly across the long, wide beach, looking for parking spaces and yearning to be seen. This form of cruisin' elicited from Paul a brilliant way to meet girls. Our usual group was five to seven, some combination of Paul, Joe, Larry, Kevin, George, Lenny, and me. Paul's scheme required at least four or five guys, a flashlight, some mechanical knowledge, a few tools, and a bunch of bullshit. As Paul had a discerning eye for pretty women, he was our sentinel. Stationing himself about thirty yards up the beach from where the rest of us lurked, he scrutinized the cars coming toward us. When he spied a car coming down the beach carrying what he deemed sufficiently attractive babes, he ran back and alerted us. As the unsuspecting girls approached, we dashed out en masse in front of their car and waved our hands at the driver as Paul yelled at her to stop. "Wait! Stop! Stop right away! Don't drive any further! Jeez, Larry, look at that!"

Thoroughly surprised at this sudden, unexpected attention, the driver stopped, and we swarmed over the car. Paul pointed to the front or underneath and claimed that something was obviously wrong that had to be attended immediately. Because Paul and Kevin worked at gas stations and were decent mechanics, they knew enough car lingo to fabricate a supposed emergency that demanded immediate attention.

> "Kev, look at that smoke coming from the engine. We better check this out."
> "Yeah, I smell gas. Could be a leaking carburetor."
> "Or a blown gasket or leaky valve. Hey, sweetie, could you open the hood? We need to look at the engine for you."

Once the flabbergasted driver opened the hood, she and her companions were trapped. Any number of imagined mechanical disasters could now develop.

> "Hey Joe, there's a dark trail behind the car, and I thought I saw black smoke coming from the exhaust. Might be leaking oil. Crawl under the front and see if you can see any oil leaking from the pan. Check the tie rods too, could be a bad leak. George, get a flashlight from Larry's trunk. Shurgie, get a rag, and let's check the oil pressure."
> "Paul, shouldn't she turn off the engine?"
> "Yeah, Joe, good idea. Say, what was your name? Could you turn off the engine, please? It's really getting hot. Don't want to risk overheating."
> "Hey, Paul, there's some oil leaking under here."
> "Crap, Joe, that's bad. So when did you last change the oil in this car?"

While Paul and Kevin banged around under the hood and Joe pretended to find oil leaking under the engine, the rest of us babbled bullshit for twenty minutes about possible disasters from driving a dangerous vehicle while simultaneously scrutinizing the car's passengers. Usually they had no clue what the hell we were doing, this being the early Sixties when most young women knew nothing about cars, and these lovely damsels in distress might have to drive all the way back to Buffalo with perhaps a seriously compromised car that considerate, mechanically inclined young men could possibly fix right there on the beach.

Eventually, we exhausted the range of possible defects in a perfectly running car. When the girls caught on, they usually appreciated, even applauded, our ruse. I recall a few times when they became furious and screeched away, leaving us in a whirl of sand. Having informally "met" on the beach, and perhaps considering us clever fellows, some girls were willing to share a phone number with the promise of a date. I don't recall if any of us ever got any actual dates from these charades—I certainly didn't—although if anyone did, it surely would have been Paul, who was suave around women. Every time we got at least a few phone numbers, it was hysterical. We pulled this stunt innumerable times over several summers, and although I have no idea whether Sherkston Beach is as popular now as it was then, one of my fondest wishes is to go back there with Paul, Joe, Larry et al. and see if we, a bunch of old men, could succeed at it just one more time. What a gas that would be!

Cars also gave us the freedom to roam the Canadian wilderness. Many a September, six to eight of us, intrepid and quixotic explorers all,

CLOCKWISE FROM TOP LEFT: PAUL FIUTAK, THE AUTHOR, JOE RAUTENSTRAUCH, LARRY RIESTER; LAKE KASSHABOG, ONTARIO; SEPTEMBER, 1963

piled into cars the week after Labor Day and caravanned to Algonquin Provincial Park in northern Ontario. We rented canoes and a trailer, left at midnight, and drove all night into the park's expansive chain of pristine lakes and rivers. These trips were my introduction to real wilderness. Never before, not even in the Muskoka years earlier with my family, had I known such freedom or such beauty. Here was nature raw and untamed—no cabins or shuffleboards, no ice cream stalls open until ten o'clock, no bells to summon us to meals at the lodge. These experiences opened an enduring hunger in my soul for wild places. Around each bend in a river, across each glistening lake, was a new world that seemed to exist only for me. Late at night, I loved to glide gently into a lake, lie back on the gunnel of the canoe, and, under a glowing sky, listen to the haunting cries of Canadian loons dancing across the darkness.

While these northern adventures were immensely enjoyable and relatively uneventful, one trip in September 1962 was unforgettable. When one of the guys

Larry had recruited dropped out just before our scheduled departure, I recruited Mike Kelly, a quintessential Irishman whom I had met at Canisius College. Why I thought he would enjoy a canoe trip in northern Ontario I will never know. Mike was thoroughly urban. He grew up in a tough neighborhood of South Buffalo, spent several years in and

LARRY, JOE, THE AUTHOR, PAUL; LAKE LILA, ADIRONDACK STATE PARK, NEW YORK; AUGUST, 2007

escaping from a Catholic seminary, drank enormous amounts of beer, smoked heavily, had been an iron worker, and weighed around 250 pounds. He had never been in a canoe before, but we needed a sixth guy, and Kelly had a thousand hilarious stories to tell about his seminary and iron-working days, and I figured he would be entertaining. Without telling anyone else what I knew about Mike, I invited him.

He drank beer all night as we headed north up the QE Way. Believing, like H. L. Mencken, that wilderness was a place to throw beer cans on weekends, Kelly tossed can after can out the car window, leaving a litter trail that the Royal Canadian Mounted Police could have followed all the way to Algonquin. At a restaurant near the park entrance that morning, Mike ate a huge breakfast, enough for all the rest of us, and as we walked toward the dock to load our canoes, Larry said, "Hey Shurgot, you and Kelly go together." I realized that because I had invited this capacious Irishman, he and I were going to share a canoe. I weighed about 125 pounds; Kelly far more. I sat in the bow, Kelly in the stern. You get the picture. For the next seven days, I labored mightily trying to paddle that canoe while Kelly, completely out of shape, paddled only whenever I looked back trying to figure out why our canoe was the slowest. "Goddamn it, Kelly, you dumb bastard, paddle!" He just sat there and occasionally steered. As Kelly doubled my weight, the stern rode low and the bow so high that I had to reach far out just to get my paddle into the water to move the canoe. While I admit that the sight of that canoe plodding along at a thirty-degree angle—with this skinny guy in the bow trying to haul this Irishman's fat ass across a lake—must have been hilarious, I got so damn mad at Kelly that I swore that when we got back to Buffalo I would kill the son of a bitch!

Mainly because Kelly had kept us in stitches all week long with his hilarious stories, I didn't kill him when we returned to Buffalo, but I was terribly sore for weeks. Every time I return to Buffalo, Kelly hauls out a photo of the odd couple in that canoe from so many years ago, and he buys me several beers at his favorite Irish pub while telling me how sorry he still is that I nearly dislocated both shoulders during our Algonquin adventure.

The other popular Canadian destination was the 3,500-square-meter Crystal Beach Ballroom. While as kids we traveled to Crystal Beach on the ferry *Canadiana* with our parents for swimming and the exciting rides, as young men we traveled to "the Beach" in cars with our dates for lovely, bewitching evenings. Built in 1924, this ballroom had become a popular venue for the big bands of the 1930s and 1940s including Gene Krupa, Artie Shaw, the Dorsey Brothers, and Guy Lombardo. Into the early 1960s, several bands still plying the dance circuit performed there on summer holidays. On several Memorial Day, Fourth of July, or Labor Day evenings, Paul and I and our dates—he with his future wife, Rikki, and I with a beautiful Irish lass named Tandy Quinlan—danced to the bands, especially Stan Kenton, until the wee hours of the morning. Enveloped in lush orchestral sounds, caressed by the cool breezes off Lake Erie, holding close in my arms my first true love, the world outside of the crystal ballroom disappeared, and there remained only Tandy, the night, and the music.

While most of my buddies had cars of their own in the Sixties, I was car-less, and during my late high school and early college years, our family's cars were pathetic wrecks that Uncle Frank labored to keep running. One winter in the late 1940s, the bottom of an old Ford rusted out, and my embarrassed father and Uncle Frank bolted a steel plate to the frame to keep out the snow. My parents seldom had the money for a new or even a decent car, and after I met Tandy, I was happy to double date with Paul and Rikki so that we could ride in one of his spiffy cars.

However, in the early Sixties, when a girl and I went out alone, I drove my parents' 1964 Chevy II, a green, four-door sedan with a three-speed manual transmission. This car was boxy and banged up, especially after the February afternoon when I drove it into a snowbank while practicing winter driving skills. For two reasons, it was surprisingly serviceable for dating. First, the gearshift was on the steering column, and second, the front seat, rather than today's bucket style, was all one piece. Thus, my dates could sit quite close—always a sign of affection—and while parked in some lonely spot, the gearshift could be left in second high on the column, completely out of the way. The front seat nicely encouraged romantic encounters, and despite my shyness, I managed to date a few attractive girls while driving this Chevy II. Not exactly a chariot of fire, but it got us to the movies, the beach, and deserted spots along the freeway.

One day, second gear disappeared. The clutch still worked, but the middle gear was gone, perhaps because someone in the family (I guessed Mother) wasn't using the clutch properly and was grinding the gears. Driving this crate became a mechanical nightmare. The challenge was to get the car going fast enough in first gear to shift into third in order to keep the car moving forward. As one started forward and the rpm increased, the noise rose to a metallic wail until the engine sounded as if it would explode, but if one shifted into third gear without reaching sufficient speed, the car bucked violently and propelled the passengers into the windshield. Conversely, when slowing down, if one didn't shift back into first soon enough, the car would sputter, shake, and stall, again rattling the passengers. While the car had seat belts, it did not have shoulder harnesses, so there was no defense against this repeated lurching forward. My dates did not like riding in this car. Cruisin' this wasn't. I should have provided football helmets.

While I was hardly a Casanova, I dated a few girls in high school and early college, but several girls refused a second date with me after riding in the dilapidated Chevy II. I cannot blame them; why risk a permanent head injury just because my car had no second gear? After Tandy ended our relationship, I wondered whether that old car was part of her decision. Alas, I will never know! After one especially excruciating evening of bucking and lurching, I asked Father why the hell, if Uncle Frank couldn't fix the transmission, he didn't buy a new or at least another used car. He said, sadly, that he could not afford to. He also told me never to ask that question again. I never did. Having to drive and to try, with Frank's help, to maintain that car for so many years was obviously painful for him, and my inability to convince girls to risk their lives with me on a date was far less important than my father's attempts to maintain his dignity as that tank sputtered down Highgate for all the neighbors to see and hear.

When I wasn't cruising the bars in Buffalo or the beaches in Sherkston, I cruised neighborhoods in northeast Buffalo, delivering spirits for a liquor store at the corner of Main and Winspear that was owned by a family friend. Then, as now, liquor stores in New York State were private businesses, and the owner of this store made a fortune. I worked Saturdays from 10:00 a.m. to 6:00 p.m. and often until midnight, making all of $1.25 an hour plus tips, driving an Oldsmobile station wagon with a terrific stereo system tuned to WUFO's all-night jazz/blues program. The liquor store was near suburban neighborhoods where University of Buffalo professors and many wealthy bankers, lawyers, and doctors lived, and could these people drink! I would deliver a case of liquor and several cases of wine to beautiful Tudor homes and get as much as ten dollars in tips for one delivery, which for me was a lot of money. I also delivered booze to many pathetic people: winos who stumbled to the door and thrust into my hand whatever cash they could find, naked men and women, drunk for days, and old people who insisted that I sign a paper labeling the booze "medicine." During every shift, I saw how easily alcohol could be abused and the havoc it could wreak. I appreciated this job because it was steady and I needed the money for school, but given the amount of alcohol consumed by my family, it was an ironically sobering experience.

Regardless of what bar my buddies and I hit on so many Friday nights, those sad, ragged customers were always present in my mind.

CHAPTER 10:
DEFYING DEATH ON THE NIAGARA RIVER

—⚏—

I met Dick Frucella in the Canisius College cafeteria in November 1961. Dick and I saw each other a few times, perhaps in the library, struck up a casual conversation, had burgers together once or twice, and one night, he gave me a ride home. By spring of 1962, we were good friends, and as our friendship deepened, he gradually played an ever-expanding role in my life on Highgate. He was also the one tragic figure from my years in Buffalo.

Dick and I came from vastly different circumstances. His father, a prominent and wealthy physician, owned a spacious home located among towering oak and elm trees along Delaware Avenue, a prestigious neighborhood. Measured against the houses on Highgate, the Frucella residence was a mansion. During one brief visit, I saw from the front room paneled walls, an imposing mahogany staircase winding to the second floor, crystal chandeliers in the sitting room, exotic vases on tables, and oil paintings adorning the walls. I thought I had walked into the foyer of an art gallery.

Dick was several years older than I and he worked as a highly paid engineer for Ford Motor Company, as he did later for several years in Detroit. Given his father's wealth and his position at Ford, Dick used his wealth to impress others. Although he was generous with his money, he was also lonely. The more time I spent with him, the more I became convinced that he had not made friends early in life and that he and his parents were not emotionally close. Because of these convictions, and my belief that he was desperate for lasting friendships, I reached out to him in ways that led to an exciting and bizarre relationship.

By the summer of 1962, he had met my friends Paul, Joe, and Larry, and he believed that we afforded him an opportunity to hang out with a bunch of guys in ways that he probably had not experienced previously. We four had known each other for many years and had forged deep bonds borne of similar backgrounds, social settings, and educational interests. Sometime that summer, as a way of trying to bond with this new group of friends, Dick introduced us to his most expensive and most dangerous toy: a fifteen-foot speedboat propelled by twin 125 hp Mercury outboard engines. Twin! Dick's idea was that we would form a waterskiing club, and as he already owned the boat, he bought several pairs of water skis and asked us to contribute gas money. Having agreed to a night of skiing, we met at my house about 5:00 p.m. and piled into Dick's car—a Ford Falcon convertible, top down—and we raced to the Buffalo Yacht Club on the Niagara River through stop signs and yellow (and occasionally red) lights. He was forever in a hurry! The five of us jumped into his boat, threw in the water skis, and roared hell bent for leather several miles into the middle of the river where we commenced a thrilling but brainless adventure.

The Niagara River is wide, deep, and fast. The average discharge of the river, the volume of water transported in a set amount of time, is 204,800 cubic feet per second (CFS). That's greater than the Columbia River along the Washington-Oregon border and the Fraser River in Canada. The Niagara is also cold. Although most Buffalo summers were scorchers, Lake Erie, from which the river flows, was usually not ice-free until late March or early April, and if we skied as early as June, we would be in water that had been free of lake ice for only two months. We did have lifejackets, but we never thought of wet suits, and given the amount of time we spent in the river, I am amazed that no one died of hypothermia. None of us had heard the word and were wonderfully oblivious to that distinct possibility.

Because Dick's boat had so much horsepower, we were able to ski four guys at a time behind it. We tied four ropes to the stern, alternating long-short-short-long, so that as the four skiers got upright we maneuvered around each other: two guys on short ropes in the middle diving under the other two guys' longer ropes on the outside. Riding with Dick in his car to the river should have warned us what to expect on the water. He started slowly as we gradually got upright, and just as we got comfortable, he gunned those satanic engines and careened all over the river, challenging us to stay vertical. The dangers inherent in this endeavor are obvious but were never so to us. As one of us zoomed under another's rope at breakneck speed, decapitation was always possible, as were concussions, fractured skulls, and broken arms and legs if the two skiers on short ropes suddenly turned inward and collided. If we hit a wave that Dick deliberately created as he cut sharply right or left, we flipped high into the air, skis akimbo, before letting go of the rope and slamming into the water, hopefully clear of the other skiers. Dick loved crashes, so he'd gun the engines and swerve as tightly as the boat would tolerate, determined to hurl us into the river or into each other. It was glorious fun!

If the four skiers stayed up an unusually long time, the first to get tired let go of his rope and sank into the river. If the other skiers stayed up for several more minutes, the resting and abandoned skier drifted toward Niagara Falls. While the precipice of the falls was several miles downstream from where we were skiing, the Niagara River is wide and swift (remember, 204,800 CFS!), and there were several anxious moments as we searched for a bobbing head in the middle of the river. When Dick decided that it was his turn to ski, he glanced around at the other boats in the area, announced pompously that none were Coast Guard vessels, and turned the boat over to us. With neither a license nor training in piloting a super-speed boat, one of us drove as Dick and two or three others skied. Dick was a superb water skier and loved to show off, so whoever was driving was determined to dump him. "Okay, Frucella, you asked for this! Gun it, Riester! Hang on, you guys!" Astonishingly, we were never stopped by the river cops, never arrested, and never swamped the boat. Nobody drowned, nobody got hypothermia, nobody went over Niagara Falls, and there were no serious injuries, probably because we were just too damn dumb to get hurt. I don't think I ever told my parents what we were doing those nights on the river or that I occasionally drove that speed boat with no idea what I was doing.

Our water-skiing adventures lasted through the summer of 1964. Dick and I remained close friends, although during the "off season," he saw my other friends less often. My relationship with him changed radically one Friday afternoon in September 1964. He charged into the driveway on Highgate, banged on the side door, and when I came to the door, he said "Mike, I have to talk to you! Let's go!"

As we peeled out of the driveway, he told me that his girlfriend was pregnant and that his father had kicked him out of the house. He was desperate and frightened, and he drove even more carelessly than usual as we headed for Mann's 300 Club on Bailey Avenue. He got tanked, and hours later when he staggered back to his car, he was in no shape to drive. He also had nowhere to sleep that night. Ever the caring companion and having inherited my mother's generous spirit, I invited him to sleep at our house "for a few days." Big mistake! Like "The Man

Who Came to Dinner," Dick didn't leave. He lived with us for six interminable months as he sorted out his impending fatherhood and his deteriorating relationship with his parents.

I had to broach Dick's impending residency to my parents. I told them that he had been disowned by his family, probably why also, and I insisted that he would not stay long. As Mary Lee and Butch had moved out in January of that year, the back bedroom was vacant, and so Dick's moving in for a short stay seemed to me both charitable and reasonable. There was room, and I assumed that once again the old house could open its doors and take in another boarder, even someone not related to our family. Father probably wondered where in his marriage contract it was written that his house doubled as a low-rent hotel, and he must have been utterly exasperated. Mother said something charitable like "Well, Bill, the back room is available, and it's only for a few days." Father silently relented, as he always did, and sank deeper into his chair by the fireplace.

To appreciate the impact of Dick's crashing into our lives, one must translate how he drove his car and especially his boat into his living habits. First, clothes. He had more clothes than I imagined one person ever wearing. Granted, he was an engineer at Ford and had to look sharp every day, but he seldom washed anything, perhaps because he was used to having his parents' maid do his laundry. He stashed his dirty shirts and underwear in cardboard boxes in the closet of the back bedroom and then, when that space filled up, in the basement. Rather than launder his clothes, he kept buying more shirts and underwear. When he finally washed his clothes, he spent an entire Saturday in the basement and used a day's worth of hot water and two weeks' worth of detergent because he had no idea how much to use in a single load.

Second, food. Dick ate voraciously. Mother prepared extra portions whenever he ate dinner with us, and as a way of ingratiating himself, especially with Father, who resented yet another intruder into his home, once or twice a week Dick bought large amounts of food on the way home from work and took over the kitchen to prepare it. However, never having had to cook for himself and knowing nothing about how to prepare food, as a chef he was calamitous. His favorite food was steak, and when he appointed himself chef de jour, he charged into the house, commandeered the kitchen table, and pulverized several pounds of steak with a meat cleaver—"I want to make sure it's nice and tender"—until there was no texture left and blood was splattered all over the table and the walls. Having hammered the meat, he then overcooked it. The kitchen filled with smoke, and the meat came out of the oven charred and shriveled. While gloating over his culinary creations, he served the barely recognizable blob with French fries that he forgot to reheat, and in utter lunacy, he insisted that ketchup was the right garnish that the meal needed to make it delectable. Mother, ever charitable, tolerated his efforts; Father detested the barely digestible mess.

Dick also talked loudly through every meal. He pronounced our surname "Zurgot," so as Father struggled to chew the charred leather, Dick bellowed, "Hey, Mr. Zurgot, how do you like the steak? I cooked it just the way you like it." My beleaguered father, reluctant to complain, mumbled something about it being "good" and silently endured. What Father should have done was hurl the whole ketchup-soaked concoction across the table at Dick's head and throw him out of the house, but he never did. Like the parades that Mother insisted we attend, Dick's residence at Shurgot's Extended-Stay Motel and his dinner disasters became another trial in Father's marriage about which he seldom complained.

Standing in the kitchen after the meal, washing dishes and wiping blood off the walls, Dick bellowed, "I think Mr. Zurgot enjoyed the steak. I think he is starting to like me!" No statement was ever further from the truth.

Because Mother detested peace and quiet, she enjoyed having Dick around the house and thought his antics hilarious. Father despised him, and the longer Dick stayed, the more Father resented his intrusion into the humble abode that he pretended was his castle. Whenever Dick joined Father to watch TV in the living room after dinner, he feigned interest in what Father was watching to establish some dialogue.

"Is this a John Wayne movie? I love his movies."

"No, Dick, this is *Gunsmoke*. It's not John Wayne."

"Oh, so this is a Western, right?"

"Well, I guess that is what it's called. It's set in the west."

"So bunches of Indians and bad guys and lots of shooting. I see. Good! Is this on every night? Who's that guy with the badge?"

"Dick, it's just on Wednesdays. It's a weekly program. The guy with the badge is the Marshall, Matt Dillon. The other little guy is his sidekick, Chester. Now I'd like to hear this. It's one of my favorite programs."

"Okay, good, let's watch it together!"

Five minutes later, Dick was fast asleep and snoring loudly, and another evening, one of many, was ruined. Father jumped off his chair, hurled the paper to the floor, and stomped upstairs, loudly cussing the jerk who had invaded his home. Given her Irish hospitality and generosity, Mother apologized for Dick and quashed Father's plans to poison him. Hospitality and generosity are fine Christian virtues, but in her fervor to save lost souls, I think Mother risked a violent backlash from Father, whose passivity and patience were severely strained during Dick's lengthy stay on Highgate.

Dick's girlfriend had their baby, but they did not marry, and I never heard from him about the child. I assume it was put up for adoption. Dick lived with us until late November and then moved to Detroit to take another executive position with Ford. (He left several boxes of shirts and underwear in the basement. Pity that the ragman was no longer roaming the neighborhood; he could have had quite a haul.)

By the time my parents moved to Canton in the summer of 1966, Dick had married and settled down. Remembering their help during a difficult period in his life, he was generous toward them. Shortly after my parents moved into an old, brick farmhouse on Tuscarawas Boulevard, Dick drove to Canton one weekend with a fluffy, white-and-grey puppy that grew into a 110-pound sheep dog that Mother named Lancer. Dick was thrilled with his own generosity, especially because he knew that my parents had always liked dogs. "Hey Mr. Zurgot, how do you like the present I brought you?" My parents loved Lancer, even though he shed all over the house and shared the premises for two years with lovable old Brandy.

Dick also bought a single-engine Cessna, and in the fall of 1967, he flew to Canton, picked up my folks, and flew them to Lansing for a Michigan-Michigan State football game. Dick loved that plane and often flew to Canton to visit his adopted parents. Mother always said that he was careful and conscientious when he flew, quite unlike how he drove his car and, though I never told her this, his speedboat.

In November 1971, while approaching Detroit, Dick's plane hit power lines, crashed, and burned. His last transmission was "Oh oh, I'm in trouble." No one knew what went wrong, or, if anyone did know, we never heard. There wasn't much of Dick left to bury. At the wake, his casket remained closed. He lived recklessly and ironically died in the one machine that he piloted carefully. He should have crashed years before running through stop signs and red lights on Niagara Falls Boulevard or gunning through waves in stupidly tight turns with 250 hp pushing that speedboat well past the laws of physics. He plowed through life in the few years I knew him, and though our time together was short, it was vivid. I can still see us roaring into the sunset on the Niagara River, defying death as we crisscrossed under those ropes, determined to ski faster and longer every night. Zooming over the water, laughing wildly, none of us dreamed that death would so soon—or so hideously—claim one of us.

CHAPTER 11:
LATER

—ɯ—

I left Buffalo in August, 1965 because I had been there too long. I spent the next two years pursuing a master's degree in English Literature, the pleasures of fine dishes such as caviar and yogurt, and (with unparalleled incompetence) several women at the University of Minnesota in Minneapolis. Tandy was long gone, I think with a sailor boy. One Sunday in April 1966, I received a phone call from Mother telling me that Father had taken a job in Canton, Ohio, with Bliss Steel and that they would be leaving Buffalo along with my sister Anne. I suppose I should have expected this call eventually, because I knew that Father was unhappy with his job in Buffalo and had been seeking a better position for some time. Besides, Mother explained, Mary Lee's growing family needed more space, and she, Butch, and their four kids would move back to Highgate. My parents realized that my leaving had begun the gradual, inevitable dispersing of the family. Nonetheless, I was dismayed. Hearing that my *parents* were leaving Buffalo, and that Highgate would no longer be home, was shocking. As Mother used to say of a death, "It's not the parting that matters but the leaving." I had left the house on Highgate, and I would never return.

While completing my degree in the summer of 1967, I worked the morning shift at a student dining co-op. From 6:30 to 8:30, six days a week, I sat at a table checking in students, making sure that they had paid for that month's meals. I watched a lot of girls walk in, many scantily clad during Minneapolis's sticky summers.

I noticed a slim, pretty girl named Gail whose long, blond hair caressed her bare, slender shoulders and whose beltless blue jeans languished on her hips just below her belly button. Watching her stroll toward and then beyond my table day after day—I always copped a front and back view—was mesmerizing! Every morning, I resolved that *this* would be the day I would introduce myself and ask her to stay for coffee after my shift. Alas, I waited too long, or thought I had. On a Saturday night in June, I double dated with a guy from New York City named Mark Signorelli whom I had met at the co-op. Signorelli was handsome, smooth, and slick; he asked Gail out before I had a chance. That evening, I ignored my date, a pretty girl from Hawaii who worked at the co-op (and never spoke to me again) and focused on Gail. I watched her walk in a tight-fitting, thigh-high dress and marveled at her vocabulary. Sexy and smart! ("A wiggle in her walk and a giggle in her talk makes the world go 'round.") The next Monday at the co-op, I asked her to go canoeing with me the following Saturday on the St. Croix River. She was startled at this odd choice of a first date but must have thought the gamble worthwhile, because she said yes. She was a far more cooperative partner than Mike Kelly. On a subsequent date a few weeks later, we went to a field where I tried to fly a homemade kite, which for some reason we named "La Belle Dame sans Merci," after the lovely and mysterious lady of John Keats's poem. (Did Keats's lines remind me of Gail?)

> I met a lady in the meads
> Full beautiful, a faery's child;
> Her hair was long, her foot was light
> And her eyes were wild. (lines 13–16)

I spent hours trying to fly that kite, adjusting the tail, tightening the wings, and running harder while holding the string more tautly. She saw persistence in me, and I saw patience in her. We spent the rest of the summer together and were falling in love.

The granddaughter of German, Swedish, and Austrian immigrants, Gail grew up on a farm in Becker, Minnesota. She started in a physical and cultural environment vastly different from mine and probably expected to marry, if she did, a hardworking Minnesota farm boy. She let me know during the summer that marriage was not in her plans, especially after I showed up at her door to say goodbye in late August wearing, upside down on my head, a cooking pot that we had used at a picnic. Gail was heading for a job at the prestigious Sterling Library at Yale University, and she was looking forward to being a short train ride from Manhattan and all the cultural advantages of New York City. (Did she think Mark might be there? The bugger tried all summer to get another date with her.) She said that she would write to me on Highgate when she got settled. I left Minneapolis deeply in love and desperately hoping that I would hear from her.

I returned to Buffalo in September and taught elementary school in Niagara Falls and night classes at Canisius College. While living on Highgate for a few weeks until I found an apartment, I thought often of my neighborhood friends, Danny Miller and the Dressel family. The Miller family had moved away, I never learned where, but I located Mrs. Dressel, and one Saturday in September I visited her tiny apartment off Delavan Avenue. Her husband had died in 1963, and her son Danny had succumbed to leukemia two years later. She was thin and frail, living on Mr. Dressel's pension and Social Security. She told me that George and Paul were still in Buffalo and working, and neither had married. We talked about our days on Highgate, about her sons' enjoyment of our end-less street games, and about loss. She suggested that I call her again and said she would try to get George and Paul to visit and we could all get together. I should have called, should have seen George and Paul. We could have played catch on Highgate, rented bikes, and ridden to the green fields of our youth, but I didn't. By the fall of 1967, I was fashioning my life, as Richard White would say, into new stories.

I heard from Gail in mid-September and vigorously resumed my courtship. We burned up phone lines until midnight, and I sent her passionate love let-ters that she told me years later were illegible. In October, I began monthly visits to New Haven. I left work on Friday afternoons and drove all night in a 1964 Volkswagen Bug with a lousy heater, an errant knight pursuing a maid full beautiful. I persisted because I found in Gail the calm, serenity, and grace that I had seldom known in Buffalo. I knew little about these qualities in life. Like my namesake in Mother's Irish joke, I was seeking directions.

Recall the photo that I mentioned of my parents kissing next to the dining room table. Their poses were nonchalant—a moment stolen for a kiss. I treasure my memory of this photo because from the moment I saw it, I believed that it signaled happiness and security in my parents' marriage. Lord knows it was not perfect, no marriage is, but the photo tells me that they never stopped loving each other. I firmly believe that despite their enormous differences in temperament, they saw in each other qualities that were attractive and desirable, even unpredictable. During the years that Father worked in Buffalo, Mother asked him every evening what he wanted in his lunch, and he always said, "Oh, whatever you decide, Hon." Mother told the story that one night she decided, "Okay, buster, you asked for it!" The next day, Father found in his lunch a sandwich containing large globs of mayonnaise and several layers of Green Stamps, redeemable tokens that Mother got when shopping at certain grocery stores in Buffalo. Why Green Stamps? No particular reason. Mother was determined to show Father the dangers of indecision when married to a whimsical Irish woman, and she probably had a slew of Green Stamps lying around the kitchen as she made his lunch. One can never completely know another, hence the necessary openness to the unexpected that should animate one's quest for a lifelong partner. A kiss at the edge of a table at, what, 6:17 on a Tuesday night? Why then? A promise of romance? What might it mean? Does it matter? Only the assurance that one accepts the other, here, now, when time has given us this moment we must not miss. Enjoy this Green Stamp sandwich and think of me.

During many long drives to New Haven, I often wondered how one knows that one has met a human being without whom one cannot be happy. In mid-November, Gail traveled to Buffalo by train. After a wonderful weekend together, she boarded an eastbound New York Central at 5:00 p.m. Sunday in the Pederewski Street station. As the train slowly departed, I had the urge to reach out and stop it, for it was taking her away from me. I burst into tears. I drove home and called Mike Kelly, and we went to Maxl's for several beers. I sat at the bar, pounding my fist, saying, "Christ, I love that woman" over and over. Kelly said that the more beer I drank, the louder I got, and soon everyone in the bar knew that I knew that I had to be with Gail. I could not tolerate watching her leave.

Two weeks later, I drove to New Haven and proposed. Gail said yes, and a week later, she called me to say that she had changed her mind. Maybe she remembered me standing at her door in Minneapolis with the cooking pot upside down on my head and wondered about my sanity. Maybe she feared that we would live by a river and commute to work in a canoe. Maybe she worried about my future as a low-salaried literature teacher. Maybe the Museum of Modern Art and the shops on Fifth Avenue had proved to be too alluring. Maybe there had been someone else all along. I was clueless.

Several nights later, after a roaring drunk with Kelly, I stumbled home to find a telegram that read, "Dearest Michael, I love you forever. Ring size 5. Love, Gail." Cat's pajamas!

We married in a charming church on August 24, 1968. Grandma Shurgot came with Mother and Father, and her presence at our wedding—this tiny, eighty-one-year-old woman in a pillbox hat, smiling broadly and gripping the little black purse she carried everywhere—blessed the event. The reception was held on Gail's parents' farm. Her father, Leonard ("Hap") set up three rows of tables and chairs in a barn, with food and bottles of whisky every ten feet, and he invited all of Becker and half of Big Lake, the next town over. It was a terrific party! Grandma wooed the guests with her gentle laugh and unassuming manners. By the end of the party, the farmers from Becker and Big Lake, who may have worried about Hap's oldest daughter marrying a guy from Buffalo, probably felt that I was all right because I was related to the spry

GAIL & MICHAEL; AUGUST 24, 1968

Polish woman with the lovely, high-pitched voice.

Despite teaching in a special education program in a federally declared poverty area in Niagara Falls, as well as teaching night school at Canisius College, I lost my exemption from military service in March 1968, the year of the terrible Tet offensive. I considered the Vietnam War utterly immoral, and when Gail and I agreed in March to get married, we also agreed to apply to Volunteers in Service to America (VISTA), a domestic Peace Corps. We were accepted, and we spent our first year as a married couple working at the Tongue Point Job Corps Center in Astoria, Oregon, living in navy barracks and making seventy-five dollars each per month. Some first year of marriage! We lasted ten months and then headed to Madison, Wisconsin, where I began my doctoral studies. Along the way, the inevitable happened. Our daughter, Mara, was born in July 1971; our son, Nicholas, in May 1973. So much for family planning! Suddenly *I* was a parent!

The first time I held Mara in my arms, I promised her—and myself—that I would be more deeply involved in my children's lives than my father had been in the lives of his. Looking forward as a father necessitated looking backward, as if

I were driving a car while looking in the rearview mirror. I would be observant, available, and curious. Our children would hear their parents say to each other and to them "I love you." To this day, that phrase is the sign-off for our phone conversations, and we call each other on birthdays and anniversaries. I would read to our children, tell them stories of their parents and grandparents, of where they and I started from, of creaky houses on narrow streets, of the necessity of knowing one's history and cherishing one's memories. I would be the diligent father, there for them whenever and wherever necessary. After we bought a house in El Paso in 1977, I asked Mother to send down the Lionel train, and Nicholas and Mara helped me set it up. It was not a one-man job. We worked together to kill the cockroaches that invaded the model village we built.

NICHOLAS & MARA, 1974

Looking into the rearview mirror too carefully, I often missed curves in the road ahead. Being my mother's son, as a parent I overdid damn near everything. Whenever I wasn't grading papers, I drove the family hither and yon, exhausting Gail while insisting that we had to seize every opportunity to see this and do that so that the kids never missed anything. Consider the annual ritual of getting a Christmas tree. Every December while living in El Paso, I drove the family and one or two of the kids' friends all the way to the Gila National Forest above Ruidoso, New Mexico, easily a 150-mile round trip, just to cut down a live Christmas tree. My colleague, Phil Gallagher, told me that I was nuts. Why not buy a tree at the high school lot three blocks away? Well, because driving to the mountains was an adventure!

For several years after we moved to Seattle in 1982, we took Mara's friend Stephanie, Nick's buddy Josh, and our big black retriever, George, and drove through pouring rain to Mt. Rainier National Park where the rain became snow.

I plowed our Volvo through rutted roads to a secluded spot where we cut down the perfect Christmas tree and engaged in epic snowball fights. Shivering in the rain and snow, Gail asked if perhaps next year we could get our tree at the lot four blocks from home. Maybe.

I faithfully attended Mara's gymnastic events and Nicholas's soccer matches and Little League baseball games. In El Paso, I took Mara to lessons at Sun Academy across the border into New Mexico, and I traveled with Nick's soccer team to games as far west as Las Cruces. When his coach could not make practice, I volunteered and later coached the team myself because no other dad volunteered for the job. In Seattle, beginning in 1983, Gail and I shelved canned goods on midnight shifts and on New Year's Day took inventory at local supermarkets to raise money for Mara's gymnastic team. For five years, one of us drove her to practice at the University of Washington three times a week, and we were in the stands when Mara's team at Roosevelt High School won the city championship. I attended dozens of Nick's Little League games and was there when his team won its division title.

For four years in Seattle, I was the assistant coach for Nick's soccer teams, first the Panthers and then the Rounders, which practiced twice a week and had matches every Saturday for most of the autumn and winter. Standing around in a hard, horizontal rain in late November while eleven-year-old boys splattered and slithered through the muck chasing a soccer ball can test the patience and sanity of any man, but I remembered too many crew races that my father missed to abandon my post.

NICK HOLDING BALL, DAD AS ASSISTANT COACH

As if channeling my mother's spirit, I sought adventure for our kids everywhere. In the summer of 1981, Gail and I took them down through Mexico's mammoth Copper Canyon on the most dangerous train ride we ever experienced. Somewhere along the route, about a hundred miles from Los Mooches, a brakeman came through our car, told us to move into the car ahead of us, and, for no apparent reason, promptly uncoupled our car. Never mind our first-class tickets. We spent the next hundred miles jammed into a passenger car filled with drunken Mexican baseball players who wanted to hold on their laps the little gringo kids as the train creaked and swerved down one of the steepest railroad tracks in the world. One failed brake, one broken coupler—Mother would have loved every minute of it!

Like my parents' trips to Muskoka, I deemed our family expeditions to the mountains of New Mexico and Washington State essential to the livelihood of my children. While in Texas, we vacationed in New Mexico's White Mountain Wilderness where the kids got their first taste of outdoor camping, and in Washington, we backpacked into the North Cascades and Olympic Mountains. Never mind the long, steep climbs to our campsites, the heat and snakes in New Mexico, and the rain and cold in Washington. What mattered was getting out there. Think what hiking with a twenty-pound pack in the pouring rain for five hours up to Seven Lakes Basin in Olympic National Park could *do* for you!

Sometimes I went too far. For two consecutive summers in the late 1990s, I convinced Gail that we should spend a weeklong vacation, including our anniversary, perched on a ledge over a roaring waterfall at the Thornton Lakes campground off Highway 20 in North Cascades National Park. ("Just the two of us," I said. "Our anniversary! Sex by starlight! How romantic!"). Middle of damn nowhere, rained like hell seven days and seven nights both times. We stayed cocooned in our own sleeping bags inside the tent and got up only to cook or pee.

> "Michael, did you check the weather forecast? Is this rain supposed to last much longer?"
>
> "No. I don't know."

The rides home were quiet, with the heat up full blast. Romantic my foot! The ski lodges at Stevens Pass and Mt. Baker nestled among the towering firs in the Cascade Mountains were more-crowded versions of that cabin overlooking Lake Muskoka. The mountain air was crisp and cold, the forests enchanting, the skiing terrific and glorious at night, the fireplace cozy and warm. Between the snoring and the screaming kids in the men's and women's dorms, no one got much sleep. Gail silently endured and asked on the way home if maybe this season one ski trip would suffice. Maybe.

For all my efforts at parenting, I sometimes failed. At UCLA, Mara became the third-generation Shurgot to be a coxswain. In the spring of 1992, her varsity eight competed for the National Collegiate Athletic Association Division 1 women's rowing championship. After her crew qualified, she called to tell me that they would race for the title the following weekend in Los Angeles. She was so proud to be continuing the tradition started by her grandfather back at the West Side Rowing Club and excited to be rowing for a championship! What she wanted to hear from me in that phone call was that, come hell or high water, I would be there next Saturday to see her race. Short notice, yes, but here was my daughter competing in the only sport in which I had achieved any success and which I had desperately wanted my father to witness. I did not fly to Los Angeles. Too many papers, too expensive a plane ticket, no accommodations—all lousy excuses. I just didn't go. How quickly one forgets.

When Nicholas and I played catch, I always wore a Boston Red Sox cap, and he wore a Baltimore Orioles cap. (I refuse to believe that the Dodgers now play in Los Angeles, and I still love underdogs.) Nicholas learned early the importance of the baseball cap and its near-magical powers to transport one toward the big leagues in a simple game of catch. As in my Dodgers cap I had fielded sharp grounders like Jackie Robinson, so Nick snared screamers to third like his favorite player, the Orioles' Brooks

UCLA Women's Senior eight, 1992; Mara coxswain, second from left

Robinson, arguably the best defensive third baseman in baseball history. In this minimal form, as John Updike insists, baseball partakes of the mythical, and to participate in this realm, the cap is essential.

In the summer of 1985, Nicholas traveled to Minnesota with Gail and Mara to visit Gail's parents. While there, he bought an official, commemorative 1985 All-Star Baseball Game cap. It was red, white, and blue, made of plastic and cotton, and bore an American flag on the inside seam. On the front, it had a star, the numbers 1985, and the words "All-Star Game" and "Twins." When Nick returned to Seattle, he proudly gave it to me, reminding me that it was an "all-star cap," not just any baseball cap, more special than even a Brooklyn Dodgers cap.

I spent most of that summer painting the house, inside and out; I even painted the damn garage. During this exercise, I wore several hats, and for reasons I will never understand, I wore the All-Star Game cap while painting Mara's bedroom, ceiling included. Late one afternoon, I laid the cap on the kitchen table while drinking a beer, and Nick noticed paint on the top. "Dad," he protested, "that's an all-star cap!"

He was crushed. I had desecrated this talisman of the game that I taught him to love. He could not become an all-star ballplayer wearing that paint-splattered cap

MARA'S GRADUATION FROM
UCLA; JUNE, 1993

while playing catch in the alley next to our house. What had I done to the imagination of a sensitive, twelve-year-old boy who had thought so hard about a souvenir for his dad from the site of the all-star game? As I tried to enter the world of my father's athletic excellence, so Nicholas realized the talismanic value of that all-star game cap. How simple a gift, how profound its meaning, how devastating its defilement.

At times, I failed our children. I was hardly the perfect father I promised myself

I would be the first time I held Mara in my arms. However, I was mostly present for and attentive to them during their formative years, especially in Seattle. I think that I gave each of them ample time, in both their academic and athletic activities, and I pray that each believes I was fair to them, that I was "there" and "around" when they genuinely needed me—as my father was generally not for his children. Parenting is devilishly difficult, and no one ever gets it absolutely right, although there are degrees

NICHOLAS'S GRADUATION FROM
HARVARD; JUNE, 2002

of success and failure. Now in my seventieth year, with three grandchildren blossoming a thousand miles away, I watch my son parenting and wonder whether and to what degree he will emulate his father in this most challenging and rewarding human endeavor.

CHAPTER 12:
GOING HOME

—ɯ—

Sport is an instrument for vision, and it ever seeks to make the common—
what we see, if we look—uncommon. Not forever, not impossibly perfect,
but uncommon enough to remain a bright spot in the memory, thus creating a
reservoir of transformation to which we can return when we are free to do so.
A. Bartlett Giamatti, *Take Time for Paradise* (p. 15)

At 3:36 p.m. Eastern Standard Time on October 13, 1960, in the bottom of
the ninth inning of the seventh game of the World Series at Pittsburgh's Forbes
Field, Bill Mazeroski hit a 1-0 fastball from Yankee pitcher Ralph Terry over the
left-center field wall to win the baseball championship for the feisty Pirates. It is
still the only walk-off, bottom of the ninth, seventh game, World Series winning
home run in baseball history.

That afternoon I clustered with a group of fellow Canisius High School
seniors midway down the walkway from the huge, blue doors of the main
entrance. Standing in the middle of our group was a kid with a small transistor
radio, and as Mazeroski came to bat in the ninth, we were hushed and fixated
on the moment. Several kids had been following the game since its start via the
small radios they smuggled into class and listened to under their jackets, and as
runs scored, they passed notes around the class about who hit what when, the
score, and who was pitching. (Like our immigrant fathers, we loved baseball.)
Our Jesuit teachers, baseball fans themselves, pretended not to notice, especially in the late innings, but outside, we turned up the volume on the radio so
that everyone heard the broadcast.

As Mazeroski smashed Terry's second pitch, the voice of NBC announcer
Chuck Thompson rose to match the flight of his staggering blast. With Thompson's
exclamation, "It's over the fence—home run! The Pirates win! The Pirates win!"

the group exploded in joy. Here was a *real* miracle! The Pittsburgh Pirates had beaten the arrogant, invincible Yankees! We danced around the walkway hurling coats and books in the air, ecstatic in this sudden gift from the baseball gods to Yankee haters everywhere. Meathead Mel Allen must have been devastated! It was 1955 and 1957 all over again—when first the Brooklyn Dodgers and then the Milwaukee Braves defeated the Yankees in the World Series—except that this time, the hero was a scrappy Polish guy with my father's first name.

As we pranced down Delaware Avenue, I imagined the scene at Forbes Field: Mazeroski, never known as a power hitter, mobbed by teammates, fans, and the press as his home run catapulted him into baseball immortality. In an instant, Mazeroski, who like the Dodgers' Jackie Robinson played second base, had become a hero, and during the bus ride home, the more I thought about his feat, the more amazing and prophetic it seemed. The world was blessed by a startling event that once again lifted baseball into that mythic realm where daring men overcame gigantic odds. If in such an astonishing manner the Pittsburgh Pirates, for whom I rooted passionately, beat the despised New York Yankees, and if the game-winning home run came from so unlikely a player, *anything* seemed possible in my life! I might never have a box of medals to show my children, but Mazeroski's heroics convinced me that I might succeed elsewhere if I just believed in myself. Maz and Jackie would take care of second base.

In his brilliant essay, "Baseball as Narrative," A. Bartlett Giamatti describes the essential narrative of baseball as the quest to return home. Baseball is "… the story of going home after having left home, the story of how difficult it is to find the origins one so deeply needs to find. It is the literary mode we called Romance" (p. 90). Like the wandering Greek hero Odysseus, the baseball player (like a kid delivering the morning paper) begins at home—i.e., home plate—and his quest is to return there, to "round the bases" despite the dragons in the playing field who seek to end his quest, to "put him out" before he completes his journey. Going home means reintegration with those he left behind in the safety of the dugout after successfully eluding all obstacles.

These sketches are also about going home—to where I started—and have been a search for "the origins one so deeply needs to find." I have strayed far from Highgate Avenue, and I will never live there again, but I realize that Mazeroski's home run was what memoir writers call a "pivotal event" that significantly alters one's life. How deliciously ironic that a baseball player's heroics could convince me that my life could be what I wanted it to be and that a life full of books and reading and writing could lead me home to find again those I left behind. And to find myself.

Giamatti writes:

> Home…is a state of mind where self-definition starts; it is origins—the mix of time and place and smell and weather wherein one first realizes one is an original, perhaps *like* others, especially those one loves, but discrete, distinct, not to be copied. Home is where one first learned to be separate and it remains in the mind as the place where reunion, if it ever were to occur, would happen. (pp. 91–92)

Perhaps one writes a memoir because one desires that reunion. Knowing that it cannot happen because too much time has passed and too many people have died, one recreates that place in words that allow one to relive memories and to believe that from where one started has followed a life worth living and remembering. I have sketched here the childhood that for many years I chose not so much to forget as to ignore. I did not realize that the personal and professional self-fashioning in which I have engaged for the past fifty-plus years, that process that, as Richard White insists, yields finally a coherence, needed these stories from Buffalo so urgently. Now I know.

I think of the house on Highgate and my bedroom in the attic, and questions flood my mind. What is the fate of a room that one's father built when others own the house? Does the room look the same? Who lives in it now? A son? A daughter? Is it providing shelter from storms, a place of study for an aspiring student? Can the occupant recognize its careful design? Imagine it rising from the floor of the attic? Comprehend the craftsmanship of this "one-man job?" Appreciate what that phrase means? Does a large dog sleep at the foot of the bed? Does a child gaze out the window and see Thomas's eternal snow glistening in the moonlight? Is the room even occupied? Is it perhaps just a storeroom? Is it still standing?

What have I brought from that room to my later life? Delicious memories of long winter nights when only Brandy and I were awake, and the world slowed to sense the stillness and the cold. A need for solitude, a place away from the inevitable tumult of family to read, write, and reflect. With many fewer nights ahead of me, every moment of stillness and privacy is precious. I wonder if the Little People still visit the old house and filch vegetables from the root cellar all winter long. Are they no longer welcome? Are the stories that animated them no longer told?

In September 1967, while waiting to hear from Gail in New Haven, I visited my parents in Canton. I spent lots of time with Brandy, taking him on walks and throwing balls and sticks for him to chase in the backyard. About 5:00 p.m. on Sunday, I packed my bag, gathered up some fruit that Mom had given me to take back to Buffalo, and walked to the backyard where I had parked my VW Bug. I put my bag and the fruit in the back seat, and, leaving the passenger side door open, walked back inside the house to kiss my parents goodbye.

When I returned to the car moments later, Brandy was sitting on the passenger seat. He *knew* I was returning to Buffalo, and he wanted to go home. He remembered the gangs of kids on their bikes in front of our house, the baseball games in the green fields, and mostly, I am sure, all those winter mornings delivering the *Buffalo Courier-Express* when only he and I dared go forth through the snow upon snow because he knew the way.

I could not take him. Mary Lee had a large German Shepherd at home on Highgate, and there was no room for Brandy. I looked at him, snapped my fingers, and pointed down. Brandy rose on his front legs, lowered his ears, and with the saddest expression I have ever seen on a dog's face, stepped out of the car. I walked him back to the house and told Mother what had happened. She said sadly, "He just wants to go home."

I said, "Yes, I know, but I can't take him."

I held him, scratched him behind his ears one last time, and left. My heart was broken, and I'm sure that Brandy's was too. Driving to New Haven to court Gail had become the prelude to creating a new family that would enliven a new home.

Surely a man must leave his father and mother and cling to his wife, but just as Brandy remembered the old house on Highgate, so now have I.

Epilogue:
September 2010

—ɯ—

We shall not cease from exploration
And the end of all our exploring
Will be to arrive where we started
And know the place for the first time.
T. S. Eliot, "Little Gidding," *Four Quartets*

Gail and I returned to Buffalo in September 2010 to visit family and friends and to collect photos from Mary Lee, from the archives of the *Buffalo Courier-Express,* and from my high school yearbooks. The day after I arrived, my niece, Jennifer, drove me around town to visit some of the sites that appear in these sketches. We drove to what had been our parish church, Saint Aloysius Gonzaga, and the elementary school from which I graduated in 1957. While the church is still functioning, unbelievably the school is closed and shuttered. How is that possible? Where have all the children gone? As I walked the grounds memories crowded my mind: countless Christmas Masses at midnight in the warm, sensuous church; my first communion; serving Sunday High Mass with its Latin prayers, rituals, and ringing bells; walking to and from school in all manner of weather; the crowded classrooms, and the strict Sisters of Saint Joseph in their black-and-white habits that we called "penguin suits." How could such a vibrant school close?

We headed down Eggert Road, turned left onto Highgate, and drove through the old neighborhood. All is changed. The Polish, Irish, Italian and German families I knew are all gone, primarily to the suburbs east of the city, and the residents are primarily Latino and African American. As opposed to Saint Al's, PS 80—now called Highgate Heights Elementary—has been refurbished and thrives. Alas, the cinder field where I tried vainly to play softball and was always chosen last is now a parking lot. Most of Highgate's trees are gone, victims of the October 2006 ice storm that killed thousands of trees throughout the area. Without the enveloping oak and maple canopy, Highgate looks barren, yet another image of Buffalo's "phosphorescence of decay." No ice man cometh, no thundering coal truck, no rag man. Do their sounds echo up and down the block? Like many of the houses, 490 looks a bit ragged, yet I wish its new owners well. Perhaps children gather in front of the house to head out on youthful adventures. The *Courier-Express* is no more; on winter mornings, do tracks of a small boy and his dog strangely appear in the snow, marking a frigid journey?

We turned right on Bailey, following our bicycle route to the green expanse that in our imaginations we transformed into a baseball diamond. Dormitories, a parking lot, and a transit center now cover our field of dreams. Jenny drove me to some memorable landmarks. The corner of Fillmore and Delavan, where Shurgot's Service Station stood, is now part empty lot and part a Kentucky Fried Chicken outlet, and the building that housed Strinka's is dilapidated and empty. Dubel's, and Paddy and Mike's favorite watering hole, Mann's 300 Club, closed decades ago. Maxl's, where after watching Gail's train leave I proclaimed undying love for her, is also gone, the victim of a suspicious fire probably set for insurance money. Only weeds remain. Like many of our hangouts on South Shore Drive, Lerczak's folded years ago. Such changes are expected, yet I wonder: late at night, do ghosts wander back looking for these haunts?

We drove to Canisius High on Delaware Avenue. Despite the significant drop in the city's population, the school's enrollment remains steady. During the two hours I spent in the library, several classes came through for a research lesson, and I was pleased to see many African American and Latino students, evidence of racial integration that I never saw there. I thumbed through yearbooks from 1957 to 1961 and found familiar images: the skinny freshman in the spring of 1958 in an ill-fitting jacket, black horned-rim glasses, and braces; the more seasoned sophomore in a better-fitting jacket but unfashionable white socks; the junior in Mr. Thompson's 3A class where four of my classmates and I who had *Courier-Express* paper routes were featured in the "Teen Time" section of the paper on March 23, 1960; a photo of the terrific 1960 champion crew team; and finally the relaxed, smiling senior of 1961 in a formal white jacket and black bowtie.

Later that week, Gail and I, Larry and his wife Lana, and Joe and his partner Gloria spent a long weekend at Paul and Rikki's gorgeous home in Skaneateles. We walked through stubble fields and woods turning toward autumn, ate sumptuous meals, consumed microbrews and excellent New York State wines, reminisced at our leisure, exchanged hilarious stories that we swore were true, and agreed that surely we would gather together more often, age and distance be damned. Maybe.

We returned to Buffalo around noon the Thursday before Gail and I were to leave. I called Mike Kelly, hoping to spend a few hours with him at his condo downtown. He told me that his lung cancer had returned and advanced to stage four. Radiation, chemo, the whole works. Maybe more surgery. God love him. He told me that despite the illness, he was still practicing law and that he and his wife, Ellen, had just returned from a two-week trip to Eastern Europe. I desperately wanted to see him, but he said that he had a medical exam that morning and then had to go to court for one of his clients. I told him I had to leave Buffalo the next day.

"Mike, listen. Don't worry. My body is handling the chemo fine. I'll send you an e-mail, let you know how I'm doing."

"Listen, Kelly, goddamn it, I better see you again."

"Mike, don't worry. You will."

Bibliography

Angell, Roger. *Let Me Finish*. New York: Harcourt, Inc., 2006.

Baker, Russell. *Growing Up*. New York: Congdon & Weed, Inc., 1982.

Berger, Peter L. *The Sacred Canopy*. New York: Doubleday, 1967.

Cornford, Frances. *Selected Poems*. Jane Dawson, ed. London: Enitharmon Press, 1997.

Eliot, T. S. "Little Gidding, *Four Quartets*." In *The Complete Poems and Plays*. New York: Harcourt, Brace & World, 1952.

Frye, Northrop. *The Educated Imagination*. Bloomington, IN: Indiana University Press, 1964.

Giamatti, A. Bartlett. *Take Time for Paradise*. New York: Summit Books, 1989.

Goldman, Mark. *City on a Lake*. Buffalo, NY: Prometheus Books, 1990.

———. *High Hopes: The Rise and Decline of Buffalo, New York*. Albany, NY: State University of New York Press, 1983.

Hall, Donald. *Fathers Playing Catch with Sons; Essays on Sport*. New York: North Point Press, 1985.

Hardison, Jr., O. B. *Toward Freedom and Dignity: The Humanities and the Idea of Humanity*. Baltimore, MD: Johns Hopkins University Press, 1972.

Kahn, Roger. *Memories of Summer*. New York: Hyperion, 1997.

Knapp, Caroline. *Drinking: A Love Story*. New York: Dial Press, 1996.

Kraus, Neil. *Race, Neighborhoods, and Community Power: Buffalo Politics, 1934–1997*. Albany, NY: State University of New York Press, 2000.

McGucken, S. J., William. *The Jesuits and Education*. New York: Bruce, 1932.

McMahon, S. J., Michael. "The Jesuit Model of Education." Edocere: Source for Catholic Education, http://edocere.org.

McPherson, Conor. *The Seafarer*. London: Nick Hern Books, 2006.

Ormond, John. Selected Poems. Mid Glamorgan, Wales: Poetry Wales Press, 1987.

Roethke, Theodore. *Words for the Wind*. Bloomington, IN: Indiana University Press, 1965.

Spencer, Hazelton, Walter E. Houghton, Herbert Barrows, and David Ferry, eds. *British Literature Volume II: 1800 to the Present*. 3d ed. Lexington, MA: D. C. Heath and Company, 1974.

Thomas, Dylan. *Collected Poems*. New York: New Directions, 1971.

———. *Quite Early One Morning*. 1954. Rpt. New York: New Directions, 1968.

Updike, John. "Hub Fans Bid Kid Adieu." *The New Yorker*. October 22, 1960, pp. 109-31.

White, Richard. *Remembering Ahanagran: Storytelling in a Family's Past*. New York: Hill & Wang, 1998.

Williams, William Carlos. *Selected Poems*. 1963. Rpt. New York: New Directions, 1968.

Wilson, Edward O. *The Social Conquest of Earth*. New York and London: Liveright, 2012.

16685303R00083

Made in the USA
San Bernardino, CA
14 November 2014